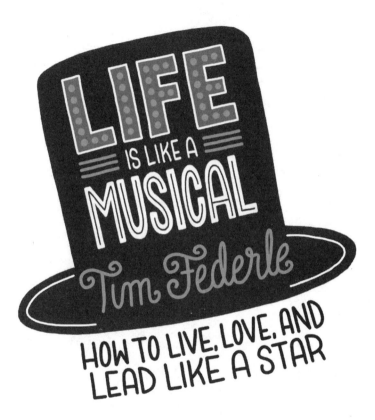

LIFE

IS LIKE A

MUSICAL

Tim Federle

HOW TO LIVE, LOVE, AND LEAD LIKE A STAR

RUNNING PRESS

PHILADELPHIA

Running Press
Hachette Book Group
1290 Avenue of the Americas, New York, NY 10104
www.runningpress.com
@Running_Press

Printed in the United States of America

First Edition: October 2017

Published by Running Press, an imprint of Perseus Books, LLC,
a subsidary of Hachette Book Group, Inc.

The Hachette Speakers Bureau provides a wide range of authors for speaking events. To find out more, go to www.hachettespeakersbureau.com or call (866) 376-6591.

The publisher is not responsible for websites (or their content) that are not owned by the publisher.

Print book cover and interior design by Joshua McDonnell.

Library of Congress Control Number: 2017943744

ISBNs: 978-07624-6264-3 (hardcover), 978-0764-6265-0 (ebook)

LSC-C

10   9   8   7   6   5   4   3   2   1

INTRODUCTION—I MEAN, WAIT—OVERTURE

illkommen! Bienvenue! Welcome!

At this evening's performance, the starring role will be played by . . . well, *you*, it turns out. So are you ready?

No worries, I'm here to help. This book contains everything I know about life, learned during my time as a theater kid–turned–chorus boy–turned Broadway playwright. Along my way to the Great White Way, I picked up tips and tricks backstage, onstage, and in between gigs—and realized just how many ways life is like a musical.

Basically, think of this book as *Don't Sweat the Small Stuff* with jazz hands.

These aren't instructions for dancing in the middle of the streets (though, by all means, go for it). It's more about "borrowing" (okay, stealing) the pizzazz and determination that define theater people, and harnessing that energy for your own forces of good.

Right around my third career transition, I recognized how many hard-won showbiz lessons applied to *all* walks of my life—not just how to be a successful performer, but how to be a successful person and partner, too. And I want you to know these insights, too.

Come on in, the spotlight's warm.

From "Cast Yourself in the Role You Must Play" (chapter 1), in which I advise you how to stop waiting for someone to "discover" you, to "Find Your Tribe" (chapter 49), in which I recommend cultivating a network of like-minded souls, I hope the advice I borrowed from Broadway can help you get inspired—not to mention get hired, whether it's in a boardroom or on the boards.

Now, you don't have to know every lyric to *Les Miz* to find these secrets and shortcuts useful—at least I hope you don't. Many of the references contained within *Life Is Like a Musical* will resonate with theater people, sure—but also with anyone who didn't think they liked musicals, until they accidentally overheard some kid blasting the *Hamilton* album. Truth is, even if you're not a diehard drama geek, there are fundamental insights about getting ahead in life, love, and leadership that only a true Broadway baby can share. Trust me.

Oh, *why* me? Great question, appreciate you asking.

Because nobody has a thicker skin or a more deeply ingrained work ethic than a lifelong theater person. We eat rejection for breakfast and still manage to smile (see chapter 40, "Put on a Happy Face"). I've worn just about every hat in the theater, at times literally—yes, that was me sporting a bejeweled catfish on my head for *The Little Mermaid*. Hey, it paid the bills.

Beneath the grit and before the glitter, I grew up swallowing how-to books whole, dying to discover answers to my own deepest questions: Will I ever be truly happy? Will I ever be cast in *Rent*?

But while I hope this book both guides and counsels you, I'm no doctor (though I *have*, on occasion, been a sort of show doctor). *Life Is Like a Musical* is more a collection of wry observations than a prescription for living—but everything here was indeed jotted down from the frontlines, the sidelines, and occasionally the footlights.

Lastly, *Life Is Like a Musical* is for people who find themselves *desiring* something—a stronger relationship or a better job or a more refined way of framing the story of their life. (We theater people call this your "I want" song; more on that in chapter 13.) I don't care what this *something* is for you. But I know it's something. Or you wouldn't still be reading. And that's where I come in.

So good luck. Or, rather, break a leg. Now please silence your cell phones. The performance of your life is about to begin.

Tim ☺

CONTENTS

1 CAST YOURSELF IN THE ROLE YOU MUST PLAY

The worst thing in the entire world happened to me when I turned thirteen years old. No, my dog didn't die. My voice changed.

For most of my childhood, I was the picture of a freckled theater kid, straight out of central casting—the kind who would someday move to New York City, of course. The dream was that once I had settled into my gigantic loft (ha!), I would, naturally, get cast in the role of Jean Valjean in *Les Misérables*. But when my voice changed, and I realized I could no longer hit that iconic "Two-four-six-oh-*one*" high note that is one of Valjean's signature moments, I panicked.

What kind of life would I have if I couldn't headline *Les Miz*?

A pretty good one, it turns out. Largely because I wasn't meant to play Valjean, and instead had to discover something more original for myself.

Friends, you've got to cast yourself in the role you want to play— no, *need* to—even if others don't see it for you. Few people are lucky enough to be born into the perfect body, voice, and era that lines up with their dream part—and I'm using the phrase "dream part" loosely here. All sorts of us have the kinds of ambitions and desires that the world is not ready or willing to grant us, for any number of

Aim your heart toward your destination.

reasons. If you're not one of those lucky folks who gets to automatically step into the part they think they're born to play, then you have to make the leap and figure out what "writing your own role"—and destiny—means to you.

You might not be a Valjean. Maybe you can think up something even better.

The comedian, writer, and star Amy Schumer has talked extensively about how people weren't willing to cast her in funny roles, so she had to create the part of "Amy Schumer" for herself. Same with Whoopi Goldberg and Lily Tomlin, who both got their starts doing one-woman shows. I find this endlessly inspiring and a bit depressing. But that's life.

How can you create your own "dream part"? Maybe it means literally joining an amateur improv troupe, and becoming so quirky and dynamic that you actually write your own material. But maybe we're not talking about just the arts here. Perhaps casting yourself in the part you want means no longer dating people who treat you like you're the hired help. Maybe casting yourself in your dream part means deciding, in your own way, to create something, every day you've got on earth. A poem. A sketch of someone on the subway. A sapling that you plant at the side of the road, just because.

When people ask me if I miss being a performer, I say not really. When I was a dancer, I was constantly on hold, waiting for casting directors to call. I was forever hoping for the breaking news that I was "right" for something—that I was deemed appropriate for a part and thus, by default, good enough. I became a writer because every time I looked at my coffee table, I saw an increasingly teetering stack of old *Playbills*—but all of them represented my past. My entire career felt like a series of endings; a show I had appeared in might have closed after seven fun, forgettable weeks, and now what? I had to cast myself in the role of "writer" when I recognized that I'd already been in enough musicals, and danced in enough choruses, and taken enough bows.

Stop asking for permission. If you can envision a destination for yourself, that's more important than the path you take to get there. The path will be overgrown, contain detours, confuse you in its terrain and surprises. But the destination is key. Aim your heart toward it and begin marching like a dutiful artist, whether you're ever paid to "make art" or not. Your dream role will likely change a few times, but the fun happens on the way to creating it.

2 VALUE COURAGE OVER CONFIDENCE

Many people are under the mistaken impression that, on a short list of the most important things to bring into an audition, "confidence" ranks somewhere between "a big smile" and "appropriate footwear." But I'm calling malarkey on that, because confidence is overrated—and courage is underrated.

Confidence is the by-product of doing something that you were afraid to do, but you did anyway. Courage is what you get *after* trying the thing you thought you'd royally suck at, and learning afterward that you only suck at it a little bit. And I'm only a little bit kidding, here.

My knees used to shake when I'd stand in front of a panel of audition judges. My voice would shake, too. The shakiest thing of all was my own belief in myself, my abilities, even my value—especially as a self-conscious gay kid.

When I was ten years old, I tried out for a local theater troupe, and halfway through my warbled rendition of *Peter Pan*'s "I've Gotta Crow," I forgot the words. Instead of crowing I was crying, and I ran out into the hallway while doing so. Now, it would have been easy to not walk back in again. Preferable, even. But somehow, even then, I recognized that if I didn't pull myself together and reach for the thing that I knew I wanted the most, I would forever live my life in a town and a place and a mind-set that was governed by fear and not fortune. Anger and not abundance. So I blew my nose in the bathroom and I went back in. Ten years old, more freaked out than ever. I still wanted to cry. But I crowed, anyway.

People, you've got to crow anyway.

When I worked on the choreographic staff of *Billy Elliot*, we saw hundreds of children at every audition. After a while, their names and faces became a blur—but I'll never forget this one kid. Let's call him Ethan, which seemed to be half the boys' names in those days. Ethan came in and spent the entire singing audition holding a green rabbit's foot behind his back, rubbing it like crazy for luck or maybe some divine help. I found him so oddly inspiring: the way he stood there, nervous and superstitious and probably even wanting to leave. He reminded me of a smaller version of myself, of the kid who went back in anyway—and, in many ways, this anonymous boy put me on the path to writing my first novel. I became a writer because I saw in this little guy a mini-me, terrified of screwing up but knowing that the only other choice was staying home. And once you've seen the world, you can't stay home.

There's probably an activity or pursuit that you would strive for if you had the time, the training, or the experience. But here's the big secret about high-achieving people: Many of them start from a place of nothing. Or the odds are against them. Or on paper they don't have the time, or the money, or "the talent" (a concept that's highly subjective) to become this more fully realized version of themselves. Guess what, gang? You don't star in a Broadway musical because somebody taps you on the shoulder and says, "Hey! You're ideal for my show! You wanna move to New York City and have a gigantic dressing room with a window that overlooks Times Square?!" (*Note*: Very few dressing rooms even have windows, though nearly all of them have mice.)

No. You star in a Broadway show because you *want* it the most—and you get lucky, after hearing no a lot. You star in a Broadway show because, despite the crippling odds, the fear of critics, and the knowledge that a life in the arts is the opposite of secure, you know the alternative is to live a life of wishing. Not for what could have been, but for what should have been.

Confidence is the payout for attempting a thing that, for all practical reasons, you should never have tried in the first place. So start working on your courage. Start working on that tiny project—whether it's auditioning for the local community theater production, or inventing an app, or teaching yourself how to design websites.

Especially if you come from a family where nobody claims to be creative or artistic—or, worse, a family who thinks the arts aren't worth pursuing.

Here's the litmus test: If your knees are shaking, that probably means you really want it.

3 CONGRATULATE THE PERSON WHO GOT "YOUR" PART

O h, gosh. A book about the arts has to cover jealousy, right? Okay, then. It's big kid talk time.

Look, gang. Jealousy is a bit like climate change, blowhard politicians, and traffic: a reality of life. So don't try to fight it.

All of us, from time to time, find ourselves in a relationship with jealousy—but that doesn't mean we have to marry it. In fact, push yourself to congratulate the person who gets "your" part—even if it feels as if you're left playing the part of someone gracious. Play it long enough and you'll be it, like the emotional version of making a face so hard, it freezes.

Avoid Chronic Bitter Syndrome.

We all have a role we feel we deserve: from the promotion at work to the flash-mob marriage proposal that never seems to jump out of the bushes for us. Make a habit of giving a shout-out to the guy who gets the gig or the girl or the *anything* that you thought you deserved—publicly, privately, or in your own journal if you can't reach him. It's good karma. It's good business. It's cool.

Saying, "Good for you!" turns out to be, you know, good for you.

One of the rare, uplifting qualities of the Internet is getting to peer in on a Broadway star like Laura Benanti, a Tony winner for *Gypsy*, wishing a "Happy opening night!" on Twitter to a show she's not appearing in—especially when the show is starring her "rival." Likewise, I'm always moved when the "loser" of any category at the

Tony Awards is the first to jump out of his seat, and applaud the winner, aka the competition. It can be challenging to be that civil. The alternative, however, is to grow embittered. To throw your phone against your kitchen wall every time you see somebody achieving or winning or gaining something that, dammit, *you* deserve! Unfortunately, once you toss enough phones, you develop Chronic Bitter Syndrome.

Bitter is so specific. You have to be a truly astonishing talent for people to put up with brittle and angry, too. Here's a hack: Being gracious is an easier skill to master than being brilliant. You're born with only a certain amount of raw talent—but recognizing another person's unique flair is an ability you can actually conquer, and tame.

We might not all be able to hit high Cs, but we can all give high fives.

Nobody gets into showbiz (or works at a start-up, for that matter) for the guarantees. We do it for the glory. And not the red carpet glory, or not *only* that. The number of directors, actors, and writers I've known who worked tirelessly on a show, through years of dogged, unpaid work, countless readings, untold hours spent polishing a scene or a script—only to be moved aside for the hotshot new guy, right before the move to the big time? Well, that list could fill a theatrical graveyard. When you're gently screwed out of something that you invested good faith in, there are two options: Grab a margarita (or two) with a friend, find a corner booth, and quietly cry your eyes out . . . *or* take the vitriol public, online even, where it ain't going to do you much good.

Put your phone on airplane mode and choose the margarita. Have one for me.

I promise you that weeks or perhaps months after your friend has picked up the check, it'll be your turn for the competition to be envious. And you'll have gotten there with hard work, years of good karma, and the luck of a little stardust.

I don't care who you are: We could all use some magic on our way to making our mark.

4 IT'S CALLED A "PLAY" FOR A REASON

If you've ever seen a group of kids dominate a playground (or inhabit a pillow fort) for hours on end, then maybe you've marveled at their limitless imaginations. My theory is that they haven't been told their fantasies are silly, yet, so they flex them at full force. And nowhere is a child's sense of wonder more apparent than at play practice—the word is, after all, *play*.

Recently, my parents moved out of my childhood house, from Pittsburgh to Palo Alto. In doing so, they uncovered a diary I kept when I was twelve years old, at a sleepaway camp in the Poconos for the first time. The camp's focus was both sports and arts, and we campers had to choose a focus on day one (any guess as to my major?). In my ancient leather journal, I painstakingly detailed the process of auditioning for the camp's production of *Annie*. As a much younger boy, I'd been heartbroken that *Annie* contained no orphan roles for boys, as there are only so many productions of *Oliver!* your hometown theater can put on at a time. So I was over-the-moon excited when I learned that this time, not only had I landed a plum role in the camp's production of *Annie*, but I wasn't even going to have to shave my head to play the part. Yes, I was a prepubescent Daddy Warbucks.

The best part about reading my diary was rediscovering how wide-eyed and delighted I was at the prospect of rehearsing, for hours on end, in an un-air-conditioned multipurpose rec room in the middle of the woods. Man, was I young. Over time, I've learned that the minute you start paying people to do something they'd always previously adored is the moment they start checking their watch to see when their next union-required break is.

But, *ah*, to pull back the curtain on the unjaded me—hungry to put in extra hours rehearsing lines with my fellow tween thespians— was to be reminded how it was to be a kid. To put on a *musical*. In a barn! For free! To try on costumes and have your voice amplified by a microphone and feel like one of the big kids, just because a whole room full of people had to sit quietly while you cracked your way through a song. (Never mind that we kids were tragically under-rehearsed, and thus I accidentally skipped an entire four pages of dialogue during the one campwide performance, thereby killing half the plot on what would be both our opening and closing nights. *Annie* never played so fast, or so full of plot holes.)

How can you bring a childlike approach to your own life? How can you ease up on your own kids, or maybe even your own partner, about all the "annoying" ways they mess up the house, or your plans? When did all of us lose our "hide-and-seek" approach to long, lazy summer breaks, and get so self-righteous that a group of noisy kids at a restaurant drives us crazy? Check yourself. Those screechy kids are probably enjoying their lives a lot more than you are. They're unburdened by the realities that come with the territory of being a grown-up, yes—but we frequently bring a lot of that rigidity on ourselves. What if grown-ups didn't have to be so stuffy? What if you're still the same, happy-to-be-alive kid you always were, but you just got taller?

There's a reason it's called play practice. Whenever possible, try to practice playing. And never get so self-serious that you turn down the chance to break into song.

5 RAISE YOUR VOICE

Speak up. Literally. Theater people know how to make an entrance and make their voices heard. And when people can hear you, truly hear you, they're more likely to listen.

There is perhaps nothing more exciting as a writer than hearing a brilliant actor interpret your lines. A document that has existed in the mysterious space between your mind and your laptop comes fully to life when somebody sharp and professional, like Andrew Keenan-Bolger, star of *Tuck Everlasting*, breathes life into it.

The first time I ever heard twelve hundred Broadway audience members laugh at a joke I'd written was one of the highlights of my life. But they wouldn't have laughed if they hadn't heard it—and, look, if the soundman forgets to bring "up" the volume on a certain actor's punch line, you can kiss that laugh good-bye. Have you ever thought of the perfect comeback or retort while lying in bed, approximately three hours after it would have been useful to employ? That's what it's like to hear an actor's microphone sputter out right on the laugh line. In art, as in your day-to-day life, you've got to be heard to make your point.

This isn't just about volume, cadets. When you mumble, or end every sentence? With an up inflection? As if it's a question, even though it's a statement? You're sending a signal that your words don't matter, and, thus, that your feelings don't—but they do. Feelings are, in fact, the lifeblood of every great work of art. But you can't hear the song if the volume is off or the melody feels uncertain.

For any marginalized reader out there who has ever felt voiceless, please keep telling your story, however you can. Keep speaking your truth, at full blast. And for my more privileged readers—those folks born into bodies or families that have allowed them to skip many of life's longest lines—please lift up those undervalued voices around you. Be a megaphone, not a megalomaniac.

You have to be heard to be hired. You have to be amplified to be understood. Practice making noise, taking up space, and—especially for my theater kids out there—not backing down. When people bristle at you, call you a loudmouth, or don't understand why you're speaking out, point them to *Sister Act*, the musical—especially the song "Raise Your Voice."

If you don't know the musical, it was lovingly inspired by the Whoopi Goldberg star vehicle. The book writer of the musical—that is, the person writing the script, who generally gets the first pass at the structure of the story—often leaves a space in the libretto for the songwriters to later come in and work their magic. Thus, the scriptwriter will frequently draft a short description of the type of song she envisions in a particular scene—the mood, the tone, the overall "hook" of an idea.

When I was the associate director of *Sister Act* in London, I learned that Cheri Steinkellner, who co-wrote the libretto with her TV-writer husband Bill, came up with the idea of "Raise Your Voice," the roof-raising number toward the end of Act One. In it, Patina Miller, in the Whoopi role of Deloris, encourages all the nuns to stand up and be heard—to sing out, dammit. And this song was inspired by Cheri, herself, who'd been told as a child in choir class to move her lips but not make a noise. She never forgot that, the feeling of white-hot mortification that she just couldn't blend. (Folks, blending is overrated.) So all those years later, Cheri inspired the renowned songwriting team of Alan Menken and Glenn Slater to write a rambunctious group number, in which every lady onstage is encouraged to find her voice—and raise it. That song stops the show cold, every time it's performed, in theaters across the world. Noise cuts through language barriers—and bullshit, too. (Take that, childhood choir teacher.)

Do whatever you can to stop being silenced. Find your way to express your reality, your dreams, the birthright you have to own your feelings. Sing that tune to the rafters. You might be off-key, but you'll never go off path.

6 TURN YOUR
   WEAKNESSES INTO
   STRENGTHS

The irony in how much I hated being a middle schooler is that everything that got me picked on as a kid gets me *paid* now. The stuff that matters, that's for sure. My obsession with theater; my sassy perspective on life; my ability to churn out fanciful stories, quickly: these things made me a target as a kid. They're my bread and butter (and wine) now.

Theater history is packed full of people who took a perceived weakness and spun it into a strength. The reason so many dance numbers in Bob Fosse's shows involve bowler hats (go look up

"Steam Heat" on YouTube; I'll wait) is because Fosse himself wore a hat, constantly—in order to cover up an embarrassing bald spot. He turned an obvious imperfection into a signature step.

It took me a long time to realize the hidden power of flaws, those things other people think are goofy about you—like, ya know, being the only boy in seventh grade who knew every lyric to *Sunday in the Park with George* (in particular the Bernadette Peters solos). I had a whole checklist of weirdness going on, like how I recognized I was probably going to grow up to be gay, when I was twelve years old. Heck, just being below average in height, and seeing myself as a lesser version of a more evolved self I wished I could be? These things added up to my being ostracized. There were days I got chased home from the school bus by bigger kids who hated my guts. They made junior high school a waking hell, two years that felt like a life sentence. I want to reach back through time and put a protective cocoon around myself.

But there's a catch to the tough years, of course. A flip side.

A major study demonstrated that those kids who peak in middle school—that is, those children who were voted "most popular" at thirteen—generally plateau, and go on to reach fewer milestones in life. It's as if those things that can make a kid popular on a playground turn out to be relatively hollow in adulthood. Guess what happens to a lot of outsiders, though? If you felt like an alien in your own hometown or school, you've very likely gone on to have an even richer, more empathetic outlook than a version of yourself who simply breezed through the acne years.

Is there a
surprise B-side
to your list of
weaknesses?

Make a list of the reasons people didn't "get" you when you were younger. Look back at that off-kilter thing you were smitten with in middle school. The oddball person you were, back when you had braces, and outgrew your shoes every other day? Notice that kid. Interview him. Ask him what he knew about his future self that you may be ignoring now.

I spent a lot of my teens in my guidance counselor's office. Dr. Marian Orr sort of saved my life (and, to this day, texts me photos of her dog wearing holiday-themed outfits). Back then she said to me, "Tim, let's make a deal. You're into the arts, right?" I was probably wearing a *Cats* sweatshirt, so, yes, I was. "And you spend a lot of time outside of school doing shows, right?" Yep. "So, I'm going to make a plan with your teachers. And the plan is: We're all going to help you get through these years, as long as you aren't overly disruptive in class."

We shook hands on it. See, I was the class clown who liked to poke fun at authority—a trait I eventually learned to whittle down until I could use those sharp observations to my advantage. I wouldn't have those tools at my disposal now if I hadn't spent so many of those years feeling as if I was speaking a foreign language in my own country, secretly, urgently studying my surroundings until I felt like I understood the world, and my place in it, in a deeper way.

I now look back and see the naïve wisdom in my youth. I was never going to be the straight-A student who didn't question people in a position of power. It wasn't in my bones. But, as a result, I became quick on my feet and a fighter for my fellow underdogs. My entire writing career became inspired by the past. I could now tell fictional stories of people who don't always have voices.

Make a list of your own "weaknesses," those things that have long hounded you. Is there a surprise B-side to the list? If you're a grown-up, congrats, and sorry: You're probably stuck with certain characteristics that will never change. For me, it's impatience—but that's also why I write so quickly. I can't stand to see a blank page.

When Bob Fosse had a bald spot, he put on a stylish hat. Where's your bald spot? Or blind spot? Or thing that you can barely accept about yourself? Go put a hat on it, and make it something beautiful.

7   **DANCE LIKE EVERYONE'S WATCHING**

ook, I get it. I understand the cleverness of the phrase "Dance like nobody's watching." For a time, I even had it on a magnet on my fridge. Because I suppose, theoretically, if nobody's watching, you can really let loose. But guess what? That's bullshit. And I wish that fifteen-year-old me had known that.

My high school self yearned to plant himself center stage for the whole world to admire—just as long as nobody watched him doing it. During a sophomore year production of *Godspell* (in which I was completely in love with the hopelessly straight boy playing Jesus), my own mother had to pull me aside after the show to ask me if I was feeling well. "What do you mean," I said, panicked. "Well," she said, "You sort of . . . danced like you were under the weather."

I was so dang mad at her. But it was true, and she was right. As a gawky, in-the-closet teenager, I'd chosen to keep my brightest self set to "dim." I was afraid that if I really went for it, and wore my heart on my apostle-costume sleeve, somehow people would see the "real" me—the gay kid, in every embarrassing color. It's that funny thing about being a young performer, or a young person, period: You want to become your most astonishing self as long as nobody sees you stumble along the way. And so I'd slinked my way through *Godspell* as if I were apologizing for dancing in the back row. For being alive, really. That's no way to live, and no way to dance, either.

If you dance like *everyone's* watching—if you start moving through life as if your actions matter, and not only that they matter but that they're worth revering—then you get to own it when you accomplish something tough, or scary. Like, when you nail a triple pirouette for the first time. Or give an incredible PowerPoint presentation. Or walk into a final job interview and *don't* downplay whatever is special about you, but rather fully broadcast what you're going to bring to the room. It's harder to do that when you're busy not accepting a compliment, or demurring so delicately that you barely make a dent. Leave the humility, fake or otherwise, back at home.

To dance like everyone's watching is not to wait for your best self to show up. It's to say, instead: "Look, I might not be *perfect*, but I'm here—and you might as well watch me take up space."

Please, friends, take up space.

You don't have to be a professional dancer with an Equity card and a pair of tights to *dance*. Putting your whole self out there means stepping out of line and showing how you move, think, and talk like the unique person you are. This isn't about pumping up your ego. It's about recognizing your place in the world.

The good news is: Once you dance like everyone's watching, soon they actually will.

8 REMEMBER: THE SHOW MUST GO ON

There's something powerful and enduring in the notion that the show must go on. New York has endured terrorist attacks, record snowfall, and financial crises. But at 7:30 p.m., six nights a week between 41st and 52nd Streets, about a thousand people are putting on fake eyelashes backstage, and humming along to Beyoncé as a dressing room warm-up. (And that's usually just the chorus boys.)

Not for nothing, showfolk do all of this whether they "feel" like it or not. This concept—that no matter how achy or disinterested we are—we show up and "put on the play," has been tested on every show I've ever done. There was the infamous rehearsal for my Super Bowl halftime show appearance, where one of our fellow dancers, in a freak accident, fell from such a height that the production company hired a grief counselor for the rest of the cast. We cried it out. We debated pulling out of the production. Still, the show went on. (And the injured dancer lived.)

There was the first national tour of *Spamalot* where I, as an offstage dance cover, got thrown onstage for our very first preview in Boston, because one of the regular dancers had fallen off a table and twisted his ankle, fooling around on a break. The show went on. (And I gave him hell for, like, a week.)

There was the second week of Broadway previews during *Gypsy* when our above-the-title star Bernadette Peters missed performances owing to a nasty cold. Imagine being her understudy. You don't come to see *Gypsy* starring the understudy—and yet the show went on. (And Maureen Moore got a standing ovation every night, by the way.)

And in every last summer stock production I've ever appeared in, from *Annie* to *Zorba*, we performed the entire show for the first time, from overture to curtain call, in front of a paying audience—because we'd run out of rehearsal time and never got to run the whole thing straight through. Not without stopping for a costume malfunction or a missed cue, anyway. And yet, and *always*: The show must go on.

Lastly, in *The Little Mermaid*, we had a forty-foot-tall, technically complex set piece that would frequently and unexpectedly "freeze" in the wrong onstage position, during the middle of "Under the Sea"—thereby forcing thirty adult fish to rechoreograph the number around it, in front of the audience's unknowing eyes. You don't stop the show on Broadway. If you stop, the orchestra gets overtime, the crew gets cranky, and the audience gets restless. Once they turn on their phones, you can never get them back. It's better to keep pushing. The show must go on.

Of course, before the show even happens, first you have to show up. Simply arriving at the starting line is the biggest hurdle for most people. Once you're there, calamity is bound to strike, sooner or later, but at least you're on-site and in the game, able to react and rejigger, even if at first you stumble.

Is it any surprise that the quote "I can't go on, I'll go on" came from noted theater person Samuel Beckett? "I can't go on," people say all the time—at funerals, after breakups, when they don't get into their dream college—and yet they do. They must. *We* must.

When you adopt the strategy of "The show must go on," you'll immediately see that instead of an audience that's waiting for you, it's your future—the one in which you march bravely forward, even when it is, at times, more of a crawl. Even when you don't know how to. Showing up is what it's all about. Now take a bow.

9 DON'T CROSS YOUR ARMS WHEN THE DIRECTOR IS TALKING

never realized just how much you say when you say nothing at all until I stood in front of a group of fifty auditioning dancers, and saw what it looks like when they're looking at you. It can be overwhelming to be in charge. You are constantly scouting for signs that people are on your side.

When I was a dancer, I was so stressed about making a good impression that I'd spend entire auditions checking out the competition, nervously fidgeting, and only smiling when it was my turn to shine. Then when I became the person who helped run the room, I realized just how many of my physical tics had probably gotten in my way as a former dancer. I wish I'd known then what I know now about how to signal to your leader that you've got her back.

First off, the key to approximately 90 percent of adulthood is appearing more interested in something than you actually are. Seriously. So, hack number one: When you are attempting to appear at worst neutral or at best enthusiastic—especially when you don't feel particularly jazzed about something—simply uncross your arms. That's it.

Anytime you want to convey the message "I like what you're saying," put your arms by your side or your hands on your hips. This may feel unnatural, but it's an instant physical makeover that says, "I'm cool with you!" (That's all most people want, by the way—to know that people around them are cool with them.)

From an evolutionary standpoint, when we crisscross our arms, we give off the impression that we are shielding and thus protecting ourselves—because we are literally the only mammals who walk upright, and thus don't naturally protect our vital organs. We cross our arms when we are unsure, nervous, or sussing out a situation. Here's something I already know about you: When you are interviewing for a new gig, getting feedback from a superior, or simply attempting to have a "big talk" about an especially prickly topic, you probably cross your arms. Honestly, it is your body's default when you're having a complex conversation. Once you start looking for this in others, you'll realize how many people walk around with protective armor up, even when they don't want to be so closed off.

I saw this firsthand when thirty kids at a time would come in to *Billy Elliot* auditions. Invariably, my eye was always drawn to the types of potential hires who seemed like they wanted to actually, ya know, *be* there. And the surest sign that somebody wants to occupy the same space as you is this: He's facing you (and not turned half-away) and focusing on you (and not looking at himself in the mirror). That's it.

That leads to my second hack at seeming interested: Any time you subtly want to get someone's attention, just make eye contact. And don't look away. As in, don't look at your phone and certainly don't look at all the interesting stuff happening behind her. Just look at her. Particularly if it's someone in a position of leadership, attempting to deliver a message to you—or, hardest of all, to a whole bunch of folks at once. Nothing tells the superior that you respect what she's saying like unbroken eye contact. The good news is, you don't even *have* to like what she's saying. You just have to keep look-ing at her while she's saying it. That alone will set you apart.

The Broadway director and choreographer Casey Nicholaw, with whom I worked on *Tuck Everlasting* and *Spamalot*, has noted how helpful it is to him when he's giving notes, following a perfor-mance, and he catches a cast member nodding. Not nodding off. Just nodding. That's all it takes to stand out among forty colleagues. It's that silent recognition that you've incorporated the information you've just learned, and that you agree with (or accept) what he's saying. Little is as exhausting as attempting to rally a group to get on your side, only to receive a bunch of blank stares in return. Be a nodder, not a yawner.

Check yourself in everyday situations—even low-stakes interactions. Are you crossing your arms and breaking eye contact? You may be sending a signal you don't even intend—and in the theater, we're all about intentions. If you don't know what your character is trying to say, how will you know the best way to convey it?

10   TAKE COMFORT THAT EVERYONE IS ALWAYS STARTING OVER

When I was eighteen years old, I graduated high school, barely, with a 2.2 GPA. I was a slacker, a daydreamer, and a smart-ass, the kind of kid who was on a first-name basis with the principal. Having not gotten into my top college picks (wonder why?), I informed my parents that I wanted to flee to New York City to audition for a national tour of *Fiddler on the Roof*, in lieu of going to the only college I'd gotten into. (This was mere days after missing my high school graduation in order to dance in a regional production of *Oklahoma!* Though I earned Ds and Cs in high school, I was a 4.0 student in the audition room.)

To my parents' credit, they gave me their blessing to chase my dumb dream—though perhaps they understood that sending me off to get an expensive liberal arts education would be akin to tossing money at a bonfire. Anyway, my mother knew theater lore well enough that, on the day I left for my *Fiddler* audition, she actually pulled me aside in the driveway and whispered, "Pull a Peggy Sawyer." Meaning: Go be like that famous fictional chorus girl from *42nd Street*, who beat the odds and got hired for the very first thing she auditioned for. And somehow I did. (Thanks, Ma!)

Now, before you throw me a parade: This *Fiddler on the Roof* could barely afford the fiddler, and I'm not even sure we traveled with a roof. It was a nonunion tour, paying about a buck-fifty a week, with no benefits, no health insurance, and God knows no 401K. But I got hired for it. And I felt such accomplishment, I practically levitated when I received the call. Hell, I remember saying to my best friend: "I will never for a day or even a moment doubt myself again."

Ah, youth. Rather: *Ha*, youth.

This sense of deep, lifetime achievement strikes me as hilarious now. Four months after I'd opened in *Fiddler on the Roof*, I was out of a job, back on the breadline, an eighteen-year-old who wasn't enrolled in college and didn't have a nickel in the bank. Welcome to the school of hard knocks, kid. So much for never doubting myself again.

From surprise layoffs to surprise divorces, many of us feel as if we're starting at square one more often than we'd like. It's okay to take solace in this. Shows shutter. People leave. Life is about beginning again, for everyone. Just look around. It's your cousin in Ohio whose manufacturing plant shuts its doors. It's your mom, joining Tinder at age sixty-six. And it's you, too—if you stop to think about the last time you had to prove yourself. It may have just occurred this morning, if you're anything like me.

One of the reasons I value living in Manhattan is that you get to ride the subway with the stars. There's something incredibly equalizing about making a go of it on the East Coast, where everybody has to deal with equally crappy weather. You glance up and see that your favorite lead from last year's crime procedural on TV is sitting three feet from you on the train, bundled up with a Starbucks and memorizing lines of dialogue on a loose page of script, on his way to yet another tryout. Starting over. A well-known Tony winner once told me that on the night he won the big award, he had no money at all in savings. As in, zero. As in, his awards-night tux was a rental. Sometimes the most solidly "successful" people are the ones with the least amount of practical security. Welcome to the big leagues—can you spare a dime?

Consider this stark truth as you continue venturing through the world. Think about the grocery store cashier who seems to hate her job, and what she may be recovering from and dealing with at home. Reflect on the otherwise unlikable person you go on a first (and last) date with, who hauls along some major baggage—which might only be a slightly different shade than the baggage you carry around, yourself. Recognize that we're all in this together, that nothing on Earth is permanent (except for *The Lion King*), and that, if you're lucky, you get to occasionally hold tight to an illusion of a certain kind of sure thing.

What I've grown surest of is that nothing is sure—and that building up resilience is a pretty good way to prepare for any tomorrow. It is after all, only a day away.

11 REALIZE WE'RE EACH THE LEAD OF OUR OWN LIFE

Surprise: You are the supporting player, and maybe even a background extra, in the life story of every person you come across. You may even, on occasion, be cast squarely as their villain. (Or love interest. Or comic relief!) Point is, we each think of ourselves as the star of our own show. Consider yourself enlightened and warned.

When I appeared in the Broadway production of *Gypsy*, I played a very small part toward the end of the musical. My primary stage time was spent in Act One, as a farm boy dancer who also under-studied the featured role of Tulsa. As with many classic musicals, there was an opportunity for additional one-line roles to be played by the chorus—and thus I found myself appearing nightly, in Act Two, as Bougeron-Cochon—a character whose name I could barely pronounce.

Bougeron appears in the penultimate scene of the nearly three-hour-long classic show, right before Mama Rose (played by Bernadette Peters) storms the stage to belt out her lifelong regrets in a legendary number called "Rose's Turn." In the setup scene, Rose is having a blowout fight with her daughter, Gypsy Rose Lee—a real-life stripper from the Vaudeville era. Rose has spent Gypsy's entire childhood forcing her into showbiz, and yet now that Gypsy is an international success, Rose fails to see that her own daughter is famous enough to no longer need her. Heavy stuff. Perfect for the stage. It's a chewy scene for two fabulous actresses—and in order to illustrate just how famous Gypsy has become, a photographer (that's Bougeron-Cochon!) flits in and out of her dressing room.

In fact, here's the totality of my responsibilities during this scene: I'd enter, kiss the white-gloved hand of the great actress Tammy Blanchard, and then I'd kneel, snap a fake photo, and exit. That's it, baby.

If you weren't my mother or my boyfriend, you'd barely even know I was in this scene. A well-trained Labrador retriever could have played the role. And yet, one day early in the run, I was backstage changing into my photographer's getup for this scene,

Everyone's a little self-centered.

when—*gasp!*—my zipper got caught. And when it seemed as if I was going to miss my entrance, I blurted out, "I can't be late for the photographer's scene!" And I wasn't kidding.

Only an actor would take a twelve-second role in the middle of a sequence starring two warring women and think of it as the "photographer's scene." Make that: only the actor playing the photographer, anyway.

I caught myself. I howled with laughter, as did my dresser. And then he got my zipper unstuck, and I raced to make my entrance ... and not a single soul noticed one way or the other, except for me. I may have felt like the lead of that scene, sure, but try telling the playwright or the actors. Or, heck, the audience.

The next time you find yourself on the receiving end of a fellow driver honking at you in traffic, or a frustrated person tapping his foot behind you in the post office line, remember: These people are going around thinking of themselves as the lead. We all are. Not the sweetest truth in the world, but a real one; other people's actions become far less mysterious when you realize how self-motivated the majority of the world is. Is everyone a little self-centered, at least some of the time? Sure. It's called survival. We're all just trying to get through our day from the only point of view we've got: our own.

Accept this, and try not to take daily indignities quite so personally. Everyone is generally doing the best they can—even if it means they're occasionally stealing your spotlight.

12 FAKE IT

If you've ever delivered a speech at a high-stakes, heavily attended event, you know how it feels to worry that everyone can see your hands shake. But, sometimes, the fastest way to become a commanding person is to *act* like a commanding person—and, yes, there's a reason I chose the word "act." What theater people know is that faking it till you make it works both offstage and on.

When I was a teenager, I was constantly assessing other people who seemed like they had it more together than I did. I was measuring up my insides by the appearance of their outsides. In particular, I had this radiant dance teacher in Pittsburgh, named Mia. Mia had a smile that stretched from, like, Harrisburg to Cincinnati. She was blonde, she was bubbly, and I aspired to be Mia in more ways than one. Pittsburgh is a small theater community, with tons of performance opportunities for pros and amateurs alike, which means I once had the rare chance to audition for the same production of *Seven Brides for Seven Brothers* as my own dance teacher. (That's the arts, for you; you go from student to peer in one audition.) As I stood there in the audition room, my knees like Jell-O and my throat like toast, I watched Mia coolly, calmly, confidently applaud for other dancers from the sidelines. Even though she was auditioning for the show herself, she was rooting for others, too. (She got the job; I didn't.)

Later, I realized that if I could channel her brand of energy—not just Mia's positivity, but the way she stood up tall and proud and in support of the competition, even when it wasn't her "turn" to audition—I might be able to graduate from kid to adult. So I started pretending I was Mia when I'd try out for stuff. That doesn't mean I wore a leotard, or started singing girls' songs, or went out and bought a pair of heels. (I already owned a pair.) It *did* mean that, during an awkward period of my life, when I was so unsure of myself for so many reasons, I felt better when I mimicked somebody I admired. It started in audition rooms—standing rather than sitting on the sidelines—and migrated to the rest of my body, and life. Soon, everywhere I went I put a little Mia into my step. And I started getting jobs, and being treated like a grown-up, too, on the cusp of eighteen. I faked it till I *was* it.

Your turn. Picture the person in your own life who most epitomizes cool confidence. Start "doing" him. Start planting your feet, rather than swaying on them—just as your hero probably does. Have the audacity to belong in the room. And if you need more help than that, try some old-fashioned inspiration, by way of show tunes; I have a non-showbiz friend who, before any important meeting or event, belts along to the *Wicked* anthem "Defying Gravity" until her hair tingles. She can't sing, not really. She's never going to play Elphaba, the misunderstood witch with a thousand-octave range. But in the comfort of her soundproof basement, my friend tricks her own body into feeling like she's flying high. And then she does.

It's not about being the most self-assured person who ever walked into a room. It's about acting like one. So find a theme song, and pinpoint a confident character in your own life. Be like her. In theory, it'd be nice if all this self-assurance could come from within. But life is messy.

Nobody can see your hands shaking. But they can always see if you're smiling.

13   FIND YOUR "I WANT" SONG

Nearly every musical has an "I want" song—that iconic moment when the audience falls in love with the protagonist, and understands what she needs in order to feel complete and accomplished and whole. It happens about fifteen minutes into the show, generally after we've met all the merry singing villagers and perhaps a comic sidekick or two. The lights dim, the stage empties, and our leading lady is left alone to sit down on a stump outside her cottage and sing about what's missing in her life.

In *The Little Mermaid*, it's "Part of Your World," when Ariel longs to be somewhere that's better than under the sea. In *My Fair*

Lady it's "Wouldn't It Be Loverly," in which Eliza Doolittle dreams of a place, a room, an anywhere that's more desirable than her current lot in life. In *Hamilton*, it's "My Shot," wherein a young Alexander Hamilton is *not* going to give up his chance to make a mark—and make it he does. So what's *your* "I want" song?

Because, I hate to break it to y'all, but a whole lot of you are singing somebody else's song.

You're singing your parents' "I want" song—either the unfulfilled dream of their own youth or a vision for you that, *oops*, you've never had much say in. Or you're singing your partner's (or, hopefully, your ex's) "I want" song for you—the one that casts you squarely as *their* backup act. Maybe the saddest "I want" song of all is the one being endlessly reprised by you—the outdated clunker of a tune from a time in your life when you thought you wanted one thing, and forgot, along the way, that you're allowed to revise the melody.

Your "I want" song—put another way, your personal mission statement—is a chance to name and establish all the ways you'd like to change your life in order to live a more targeted, goal-oriented, fulfilling version of your own destiny.

(Hold for applause.)

Sound heavy? Remember, a lot of "I want" songs are pretty damn upbeat, like "Purpose," from *Avenue Q*, in which a puppet finds a lucky penny that launches him on a jaunty journey. Your song doesn't have to be stuffy or self-serious. It doesn't even have to be a song. All your "want" needs to be is focused enough to help you steer your life. The catch is that your song is bound to change and mature. In fact, it almost certainly should.

When I was nine years old, my parents took me to see a performance of the national tour of *Cats*. As ridiculous as the show is—Adults! Dressed as cats! Without irony!—when I learned that there was a job that paid you to wear makeup and fur, and sing at the top of your lungs, I had found my "I want" song—just like that.

You're the leading character in your own life.

I hadn't even hit double digits yet, but I recognized that my earlier years, spent twirling around in my backyard and earning side-eyed stares from the neighborhood kids, weren't frivolous at all. They were practice.

My "I want" song became: "I want to get to Broadway someday." And get there I did—though not in *Cats*, which, as proof of God's sense of humor, closed the week I moved to New York City. Meow.

And yet! Despite pointing my whiskers *hard* toward the direction of Broadway, and in spite of my "I want" becoming an "OK, I've got it now," it took me far too long to recognize that on the other side of a Broadway dream stood the reality of actually getting there . . . and then what?

The big secret is: You're supposed to write yourself a new want, every now and then.

Right before I turned thirty, about twenty years after I'd first seen those damn dancing kitties, I realized I'd rather write the next *Cats* than actually be one. So I changed my tune. This time, I'd be a writer—one way or another. One page at a time.

Please, never forget you're the leading character in your own life. Read that sentence again: You aren't the supporting cast. You're it, baby. Too many of us relegate ourselves quite willingly to the sidelines of somebody else's story, for any number of reasons. Starting today, own the fact that on the grand musical that is your own journey, you're the only person who's taking the final bow. You're the whole show: the dialogue, the inner monologues, the crew, and the cast. So start composing a life that's a joy to actually sing about.

What's your signature tune going to be? How hard will you belt it out till you get the thing you want? Not what your folks or your teachers or your former *you* wants. You've outgrown her. And thank goodness for that.

What's the big "I want" of the person reading this book, right now? Go get it. Sing that song. Sing it till you know it by heart.

14 THE REAL WORK HAPPENS AFTER OPENING NIGHT

Anybody can be good once. Any guy can nail a single audition. And yet, we fall in love with Big Story moments—the gold medal ceremony. The number one best seller. The opening night flowers. The real work happens after opening night, when the flowers wilt, along with the enthusiasm.

The trick to keeping your gig (and your relationships!) fresh is to get in the "first time ever" mind-set. To approach your day-to-day life with curiosity. Think that sounds impossible or hokey? The dancer Marlene Danielle was in the cast of the original Broadway

Cats—and then stayed there for its entire run, claiming to never get bored. Folks, we're talking eighteen years of kitty litter. "Acting is reacting," she said in an interview, once, and I never forgot it. If you amble through life on automatic, you miss all the interesting cues and signals that are around you every day.

We each have elements of monotony in our lives, sure. But now imagine being Yul Brynner, who played the title role in *The King and I* over the course of thirty years and 4,500 performances. The songs never changed, gang. It was the same show for three decades, and he found a way to keep it real—long after the metaphorical red carpet, way back from opening night, had been rolled up.

Your own signature role is you, so how are you going to keep it vital and alive? By staying in the moment, as present as possible, and open to the cosmic ironies of each new day.

When you find yourself in a position of making a difficult decision—like, say, possibly breaking up with your longtime girlfriend because of a cute new coworker—don't ask yourself what that hypothetical new relationship is going to feel like on the exciting days. Those days are only occasional. Instead, try picturing what the actual day-in, day-out might be. Relationships are ongoing projects; they are not your beach destination wedding and they're certainly not the swim-up bar on your honeymoon. The real grit is required only once the champagne has gone flat, and you're stuck with a dog to walk and a floor to mop. Who do you wanna be stuck with then? (And who would you like your *partner* to be stuck with—which is all you can really influence.)

Same goes for your career. The real efforts occur when the cameras go away and the D.J. turns off the music. Opening nights happen once. True stripes are earned on all those days that follow, when you'd rather stay in bed during a matinee; when you're fighting a cold but so is your understudy; when the audiences have stopped coming and you've got to use the last ounce of gas in the tank. A body of work and a reputation to accompany it are made up over the long haul. When you're evaluating a substantial change, remember this. All of your heroes—not the unlikely overnight successes but the true workhorses, the folks who have gone the distance one rejection at a time—know that days are made of hours, and that hours are spent on repetition and practice in order to make a performance look effortless.

If you want glory, don't play the lottery. Pay your dues. You'll be a winner the old-fashioned way, not by chance but on purpose.

15 BUY SOMETHING PHYSICAL TO REMEMBER A BIG WIN

I used to have a tradition when I initially began crashing auditions for shows in New York City. The tradition was this: If the tryout went terribly, I'd buy myself something. As in: If, after I'd gotten to the audition location—and warmed up in the waiting room, and then stood in an epic line, and gotten myself inside the actual room, and then the choreographer's assistant spent twenty minutes teaching us a complex dance combination, and I'd danced my Midwestern heart out—but despite my most earnest efforts, I'd been eliminated in the first round: I would march myself ten blocks to the Port Authority Bus Terminal, head out to New Jersey, and pay a visit to

IKEA to buy myself a little something Swedish.

This is not a joke, or some kind of symbolism. The bus to IKEA leaves five times a day, and it is always packed.

Why IKEA? I was on a budget, for one thing. And for a single dollar you can get, like, two lamps and a cheese grater. But my trips to IKEA were really a method of medicating, I suppose, that didn't involve nicotine or tequila.

I carried on like this for months, until I started regularly booking gigs. Then the trips to IKEA stopped. And, ironically, it felt as if something was missing, now that luck had found me. It turns out I'd underestimated the value of physically marking the good moments, too, and not just the disappointments.

Confession: I long ago got rid of a lot of the in-retrospect junk I picked up along the way. (One only needs so many $3 can openers.) These days, I save the souvenirs for the big stuff; whenever I turn in the final draft of a new musical or hit any kind of major life milestone (a new apartment! a successful seventh date!), I mark the moment with a significant memento. Why? Because every time I walk across my Persian carpet in my entryway, I get to remember where it came from, and why; the first Broadway musical I wrote bought it, both literally and metaphorically. Every time my feet touch those fibers, I get to say: I did that.

If you don't plant flags along the vast terrain that is your life, you run the risk of looking back and seeing a landscape that looks pretty flat.

One of the great benefits of being a full-time show-person is that

I can peek back at almost any given year, past the age of twelve, and remember exactly where I was—especially when I was thoughtful enough to keep an object from the show. I was born in 1980, but in many ways, my life began in 1992. That's when I was cast in a local, professional production of *Oliver!* at the Pittsburgh Civic Light Opera. And even though one of the other workhouse boys stole my cute costume hat during the run, and tried flushing it down the toilet because he was jealous that I had a solo line in "Food Glorious Food" and he didn't (true story!), it was still the most life-changing summer of my youth. I've got the opening night T-shirt to prove it—not to mention a framed show poster, and a signed bookmark given to me by the leading lady. These things make up a collage of my life, in living 3-D.

The older you get, the more the shows run together, and the more the years do, too—but the mementos and tokens help jog the memory. Don't populate your home with generic tchotchkes that looked good in some decor magazine. Instead, furnish your life with authentic souvenirs and one-off keepsakes that make you grin, make you remember, and make you thankful.

The one thing that both good times and bad times have in common is that they're yours. Experiment with giving those highlights and lowlights a physical manifestation. At the end of a bad day, there are worse things than finding yourself in the beautiful, slightly melancholy museum known as your past.

16 FIGURE OUT WHAT
KIND OF NO IT IS

R ejection is a day-in, day-out reality not just in a life of the theater, but in any life, period—especially for anyone brave enough to put himself out there. So how do we break down all those slammed doors—and how can we tell which doors aren't locked, but are only temporarily closed?

One of the biggest mistakes I made through my twenties was thinking there was only one kind of *no*. When it came to auditions, if I heard the word no, I thought it meant: no, forever. As in: *No, you're a terrible person, and you're never gonna get cast in our show.* (Once a drama kid, always a drama kid.)

But there are actually three kinds of *no*s in the world. There is, admittedly, plenty of *no, never*. (This one occurs on the majority of first dates, generally within the initial thirty seconds.) But there's also, *No, not right now*—as in, *No, I just got out of a relationship and you're super swell but I'm not in a place to be with you right this second*. And there's also, *No, you asked the wrong way, go away and go back with a different approach*. Your job, anytime you're rejected for something you truly desire, is to become a detective, and figure out what kind of *no* it is.*

When I was twenty-four years old, I attended an open cattle call audition for *Chitty Chitty Bang Bang*, a show that starred a "flying" car. *Chitty* was moving to New York City from the West End of London, but the producers were looking for an all-new American cast, and the audition notice claimed to be seeking dancers who fit my exact description: old-fashioned jazz-and-ballet-trained hoofers, between the ages of twenty and forty. I had this one made. I showed up early, kicked my way through the dance combination, and swore I'd nailed it—before being promptly cut by the choreographer's assistant, who was running the audition that day (and seemed to relish the power). It was a bummer. I needed that job. There were bills to be paid, and I was tired of leaving New York to dance out of town; houseplants need someone around to water them. As I gathered

---

*Disclaimer, and I'm gonna say it loud so the whole class can hear me: When in doubt, no means no when it comes to anything PG-13 or R-rated on the romance spectrum. Take people at their word, period.

my dance bag and pride that day, to take off from the audition and pick up some emergency ice cream on the way home, I wrote *Chitty Chitty Bang Bang* off as a lost cause. (And then ate half a pint of Cherry Garcia for dinner, before ordering Thai food for two, even though I lived alone.)

This would be a crappy morality tale if it ended on Thai food, right? A few months after *Chitty Chitty Bang Bang* opened on Broadway, a guy in the cast left the production to join the tour of *Jersey Boys*. That meant they needed an immediate replacement. I got a phone call from the casting director—who'd kept my headshot on file from previous auditions—saying, "Hey, we just lost a guy who's exactly your height, you wanna come in to audition for his replacement?"

Sure, I did. Those plants still needed watering.

At the follow up audition I saw fifty other boys who fit my exact bill; we were all 5-foot-7, in order to fit the costumes of the guy who was leaving. We were also all "audition buddies" in the way that says: *I hope you do a kick-butt job today, but I also hope I get this gig.* Anyway, I did what I always do: I took a deep breath and I danced my heart out and I left the rest of it up to the fates—but this time, after they "cut" the room in half, and had us sing our sixteen bars of music (which is about thirty frantic seconds of song), I actually got hired.

I was back on Broadway, baby!

Fast-forward two weeks; yes, that's how brief a time I had to learn the entire show, and have my own mini opening night. The choreographer herself, Gillian Lynne, celebrated for her work on

Phantom and *Cats* (now and mostly forever), happened to be in New York on my first night in the show. As the lone new guy, I was surrounded by original cast members who had, by this point, been performing the show for about three months. After the curtain call, Gillian tracked me down backstage to say, "What a shame you didn't audition originally. You were terrific and would have been great in the original cast."

And while I wish I could have mustered more decorum, I couldn't help but blurt out: "Yeah, it's a shame your assistant cut me last year, when I first auditioned!"

Luckily, she laughed, once she realized I actually *had* auditioned.

I guess the kind of *no* I heard on the day of the original tryout for *Chitty* was: *No, not now—try again later*. But if I'd harbored any bitterness, or refused to go back to the drawing board and put myself on the line for them again, I would have missed out on so much. *Chitty* led to new relationships of every stripe, and I'm genuinely grateful I joined the show when I did, as a replacement. The entire situation turned into one big *yes*—it didn't just get me back on Broadway, it led to the very friendships that hastened my becoming a published author. All because I'd been cut initially, and said yes when they called me back in.

Your job in life is to find the yes that is buried in the many *no*s you'll hear along the way. Are you being told no because your boss actually has an agenda—or because she really wants what's best for you? Think of all the times your parents no'd you—to keep you out of traffic, out of the way of a boiling pot, or off any number of wrong paths. Are you getting other kinds of *no*, like when you've cold-called somebody and asked for a favor on the wrong day? Don't disregard him just yet—he may have a point. Try a different way. See it from his perspective. Ask again.

To beat the odds, fine-tune your savvy about when it's time to give up, as opposed to when it's the right day to dig back in. Sometimes *no* is the exact inspiration you need to get to a *yes*.

17 FORGET YOUR RÉSUMÉ. POLISH YOUR REPUTATION

Look, you might have a mantel full of awards (congrats!), or simply be regarded as an expert (that's cool, too!), but what other people will end up caring about is the energy you actually bring into the room. Or don't, for that matter. This isn't a dig at qualifications; by all means, work your tail off to become the best of the best, with exemplary credentials and knowledge to match. But whether you're a doctor or a dancer, what the majority of folks will value most is how you make them *feel*. That starts, and ends, with how you act.

I learned this lesson when I assisted the Broadway choreographer Randy Skinner on the original company of *White Christmas*. Randy had been a young assistant himself on the original company of *42nd Street*; if anyone had experience evaluating thousands of tap dancers for only a few prime spots, it was Randy. I remember well the audition day for *White Christmas*, with dancer after dancer strutting into the room with tap shoes slung over their shoulders. From the first moment you can't help but observe how would-be hires interact: not only when it's their turn to step up and shine, but as they stand off to the sides, and figure nobody's watching them. Either Randy's other assistant or I would teach a group of about fifty dancers a forty-five-second tap combination. Roughly twenty minutes later (it all moves fast!), four people at a time would be called out into the center of the dance floor to perform the mini routine they'd just learned. But even before they began dancing, I'd already developed an impression of nearly everyone; it's human nature to begin figuring out who seems cool and who seems, well, more complicated.

What stays with me to this day is the way Randy regarded each of their résumés, laid out on the floor before him. As in, he didn't. At all. He basically never looked at their well-polished CVs, unless he'd forgotten a dancer's name, and wanted to give him or her a correction. Only then would Randy take a glance at her credentials, just to grab her name. Otherwise, he would simply watch the people dance, and, on gut instinct alone, make his decision as to who got kept around to sing, and eventually get cast.

I marveled at this. And at the time, thought it was nuts, too. The hours I'd spent as a young dancer choosing the right fonts and spacing on my own résumé! I remember pulling Randy aside to ask why he wasn't considering the wealth of experience these folks had; we were cutting people who'd been in *Crazy for You*, and a host of other tap-heavy shows, and it felt wasteful to me. But Randy explained himself, and how he doesn't particularly make note of whether five or ten years ago someone had a gig somewhere. It's all about today in the theater, which can be brutal. Do you still look as if you belong in a chorus line? Are you still willing to take corrections? More than anything, Randy seeks sturdy performers who learn fast and don't get flustered when a new routine is thrown at them. So, he basically disregards résumés completely.

This mind-set isn't just about evaluating skills. This is also, largely, about attitude. All the impressive credits in the world get thrown out when you bring a storm of negativity along with you.

Again and again, people hire the person they want to be semi-trapped in a room with, for hours on end. Folks who can maintain some humor and humanity during dark, difficult times. (If you've never been out of town with a bumpy new musical, you can't imagine just how dark it gets, like being in a jail where all the inmates are wearing glitter and panicked grins.)

No matter what the industry, every gig has those days where you don't know how you'll figure your way out. Reputation beats résumé nearly every time.

18 LET SOMEONE ELSE TAKE A BOW

Life is not a one-man show. Sometimes it would be easier if it were, but, alas. Nope. Your world is populated with all sorts of side characters, miscast and otherwise. But if you do the graceful thing every now and then, and allow your vast supporting cast to take the final bow, they'll consider you a star. A friend. A mensch, as they say in Yiddish and showbiz.

If there's an overwhelming takeaway from being on the creative team of a new Broadway musical, it's that one person's good idea is the whole group's win. The scenery can't sparkle if the lighting designer doesn't flip on a switch. You can't admire the leggy chorus girls if the costume designer puts them in head-to-toe tunics. And if the scriptwriter comes up with a particularly pithy turn of phrase that the lyricist then grabs to use in a song, it's a compliment—even if you have to cut the line to accommodate its status as the title of a new ballad. Did the songwriter "steal" your good idea? Maybe. But isn't so much of art, and being a thoughtful person, about consciously borrowing from the best? Didn't somebody once teach you how to tie your shoes, and look both ways? We all stand on the shoulders of those who came before us, whether we know their names or not.

The real stars in life aren't just folks with their names blinking above the title. It's those people who have "made it," whatever *it* is, and then go out of their way to say, "I couldn't have achieved this without this other person." Stars are people who share the trophies and salute the helpers.

My cowriter on *Tuck Everlasting*, Claudia Shear, and I could not have pulled off the tireless process of rewrites on a new musical were it not for our loyal script assistant, Angela. She'd stay up till 3 a.m., reformatting our pages and getting complex documents to stage managers, who'd in turn then pass out those new pages to the actors, bright and early for rehearsal. Whenever I could, I'd text Angela, "You're the best." Sometimes that's all I had the energy for, at the end of an eleven-hour marathon day, when you're not sure how you're ever going to crack the problems in Act Two. But there's always enough gas in the tank to say "Thank you"—or even "thx," in text parlance. Theater is a group effort. So is being an adult—at least the sort of adult others want to be around.

In your own life, where might you be better served by not hogging all the credit? Is it in small, private ways, like the way you coparent? Are there beautiful, sensitive things about your child that could only have been inherited from the other parent? Say it. Name it. Give credit. At work, do you occasionally manage to steal the thunder of someone junior—a team player who has completed excellent under-the-radar work under your tutelage? By letting others take the final bow—by making note of an ordinary worker bee's otherwise overlooked efforts—you're helping cultivate an environment where people feel more seen. More appreciated and more useful, ultimately. Life hack: That's better for you in the end, anyway.

Unless you plan on living your days on a desert island, start paying attention to all the people who help you cross the finish lines that make a successful life. It might not take you a whole lot of effort to help them feel appreciated, but I guarantee that, for them, it will be a moment front and center that doesn't come often enough.

19 BE A GOOD SCENE PARTNER

Nobody is more conscious of his breath and general hygiene than a dancer. In a career that requires you to share close quarters with other sweaty people (and get paid for it!), you develop a distinct sense of the aura that you give off. Along the way, the so-called "best" dance partners—and scene partners, in general—are generally not the most talented. They are instead the most considerate. They develop a sixth sense about the effect they're having on you, and your experience, and your space. That means breath mints and deodorant and changing your shirt if you're performing a *pas de deux* and your shirt is soaking wet with sweat. But it means more than that, too.

Sensitive scene partners, per the "improv school of comedy," add on to whatever it is you've thrown at them. Rather than rejecting the kind of energy the other person is giving off, they work with it. We call this "yes, and" in the world of acting—acknowledging a statement that's been directed to you, and then adding on to the sentiment with a positive response. We've all had work and life partners who tell us everything we're doing wrong without suggesting ways or methods to help make a situation better. Don't be that kind of partner. The "no, but" guy who never seems to help lift his partner to her potential, but instead points out everything she's doing wrong. This applies across social strata and relationship type. I marvel at parents of toddlers whose resources of patience allow them to pivot their child away from an undesired activity (*No, we are not getting every single toy out right now*) and toward another (*But look! Here's a baby carrot that I'm going to make talk in a funny voice!*). It's all about working with what you've got, even if it's an unreasonable two-year-old.

Good partnering techniques apply to teamwork, too. I've heard that in certain TV writers' rooms, staff members are not allowed to pitch problems from the sidelines; that is, if a particular scene doesn't seem to be landing, you can't just blindly say, "This doesn't work," or "This isn't funny," or "This bit isn't paying off." That isn't being a team player; that's being a critic. Instead, you've gotta suggest a way to fix it. "This isn't paying off, but if we gave the joke more context, I bet it would—and here's how we might try that . . ." Great. Now you've helped instead of hindered.

Back to one-on-one stuff. In my own experience, the golden

rule of dance partnering is this: Don't drop the girl on her head. Literally. When I was twenty years old, I performed in the *Radio City Christmas Spectacular* alongside a partner who was also making her New York debut. Katie and I radiated youthful excitement. We were Christmas incarnate. And yet, no matter how unjaded you are, entertaining four thousand people at a time for a ninety-minute show upwards of five times a day is downright grueling. Jingle bells are only charming for so long—but a job is a job. Even when you're bone-weary and zonked to the core, don't let your other half down. Put another way, don't drop her when you've got her in an overhead lift, because her life actually depends on you and your meager upper-body strength. No matter how tired you are, you have to dig into your deepest sense of work ethic and muscle out one more burst of energy, and you cannot let your partner career to the floor. It's as simple (and occasionally tiring) as that.

A truly great scene partner means something else, as well: that you will never look better than when you make somebody else look good.

20 BE EXTRA NICE TO THE P.A.'s

Go out of your way to be especially respectful to the people on the sidelines who don't have the privilege of walking around with a great deal of status. They are the secret engines who make everything hum. Not just that: Never look down on the very people who are on their way up. The bosses of tomorrow are the assistants of today, and they always remember the nice guys. Same goes for the folks who stock the aisles at your local drugstore, or pick up the towels at the gym. They remember the not-so-nice people, too.

Every musical has a whole bunch of production assistants who stick to the corners of the rehearsal studio. In the old days they were called gophers—as in, they'll "go" out "for" just about anything the boss/director/stage manager needs, which generally falls under the category of "coffee" or "more coffee." These folks are frequently just out of college, bright-eyed and Broadway-tailed and living in one-bedroom apartments with three roommates. And though they might not have a lot of measurable power in the world now, you never know who they're going to become.

That local middle school student who's paying for his after-school dance classes by washing the studio's mirrors? He might someday grow up to win a Tony Award. That's what happened to my

Nobodies aren't actually nobody.

friend and mentor Tom Schumacher, who started out in the theater doing any odd job he could, just to be as close to the greasepaint and the spotlights and the box office as possible. He was crafty, and commanding, and made a lot of connections, and he grew up and became the producer of Broadway's *The Lion King*, among dozens of other worldwide projects. He still remembers the people who gave him a chance when he was a "nobody."

(By the way, even nobodies aren't actually nobody; I'm a huge believer in treating everybody with dignity and humanity—but there's a reality to how we view the unpaid helpers of the world, and this is your encouragement to treat them as if they deserve your full respect. Because they do.)

A special note to any low-on-the-rung readers out there, right now: I was you, once. Genuinely. Before I was a writer, I made the transition from dancer to dance captain to associate director on various musicals. I've held a clipboard in shaky hands, and tried to make sense of my place in the room, and often I found myself feeling disregarded in my position as the support staff to a senior member of the creative team. Many people in the cast and crew didn't even know my first name (let alone my unpronounceable last) after weeks of rehearsals. So listen up: If it feels as if nobody is noticing all your hard work, keep at it. There are a lot of flakes out there, especially in the arts. People who fall away, fast. People who can't handle the actual demands and heavy lifting of the real world, and who are only "in it" for the perceived glamour while lacking the necessary grit. Lean in to your grit. The right people will notice you—if they don't, they aren't the right people. Not for you to populate your precious life with, anyway. If you commit wholeheartedly to your gig, and to working diligently on the sidelines with good cheer and a whole lot of follow-through, your Swiss-army-knife-like effectiveness will earn you a place at the table, and in the room. I promise.

The bosses of tomorrow are the interns of today. Not only is it the right human value to treat them as equal members of the team, it's also a savvy business technique: The first thing that assistants do when they hang up from a nasty phone call is report in to their boss—or forward the email, for that matter. Be the person who leaves the assistants smiling. Sooner or later, you might be working for them.

21 MAKE STUFF. DON'T MAKE FUN OF STUFF

Have you ever tried making something from scratch? Like, something harder than pancakes but easier than, say, *Hamilton*? It's hard. It's humbling! To work on your own, or even on a team, attempting to build a product or a musical or an anything, is to become aware of how challenging it is to take a vision and whip it into a reality. It's easy to make fun of stuff and difficult to actually make stuff.

I see it on social media all the time. The sniping. I'm guilty of it, too. Particularly in the days leading up to me writing my own material, before I was brought to my knees by how hard it is to translate your brilliant vision into an actual, actable script. And yet, we've all been sofa critics. You're watching an awards show, or seeing a new musical, or tuning in for a red carpet. And you think: How could a person be so clueless as to prattle on at the podium or design such a garish dress? Half the time this sense of judgment is residual resentment from your own efforts not being met with acclaim. The rest of the time, we're speaking from the wild naïveté of someone who has never attempted to give a speech, make up an original dance, or create a garment. We're heckling the TV screen from behind a bowl of Doritos.

I was perhaps the most prototypical snarky gay teen who ever lived. When you grow up getting picked last for dodgeball, you learn how to fight back with your words, if not your fists. I'd think nothing of watching the school play and then turning up my nose at what felt like a misfire (even though I'd been too scared to audition for the play myself). Later, I'd see touring shows come through Pittsburgh and proclaim that "I could have been better up there." When I was seventeen. Watching *Les* friggin' *Miz*. I roll my eyes at that little Tim now. Because, having now written my own shows, half a lifetime later—not to mention screenplays and books (and dating profiles, oh, the dating profiles)—I know just how hard it is to get anything right. Particularly when it's your heart that's on the line. It's tough to make stuff people like. Hell, it's tough to make stuff *I* like.

This isn't about not being critical. Observing your otherwise competent boss completely bungle a new product launch is an opportunity to reflect upon how you might have approached it differently.

But talk is cheap. It isn't until you're facing a boardroom full of employees that you realize how hard it is to make things look easy. In a broader sense, anyone who has ever stared down the blinking cursor of a blank page can appreciate how extraordinary it is for any piece of art, let alone a hit musical like *Dear Evan Hansen*, to make it to Broadway. That show—a completely original idea in an age of branded reboots, about a modern teenager who finds himself at the middle of an unintended social media maelstrom—sprang from a couple of writers' brilliant, ambitious minds, and went on to play to audiences held in rapture, all the while being supported and guided by dozens of people backstage, from wardrobe crew to techies. None of them would have gigs now if the show's creators had only sat around *talking* about how smashing their show would be someday. They had to actually make the thing.

How easy it is, when the lights come up at any given intermission, to say, "God, this sucks." It's so much harder to sit with the thought: *Gosh, I wish this were better.*

The truth is, nobody sets out to make a terrible thing. Including you. Even if your "thing" never becomes everyone's thing, your appreciation of fine work will deepen—but only if you stop criticizing from the sidelines, and start contributing.

22 CREATE A NEW FAMILY FROM YOUR CAST

Next time you find yourself approaching a family gathering with some trepidation—not to mention any potentially "loaded" holiday—try to go into it with the mind-set of a theater performer, who generally only gets one day off at a time. Only so much can go wrong, I've learned, when you've just got twenty-four hours to celebrate something. A lot can go right, though—even when you don't end up with any family time, at all.

The first time I missed a Christmas at home, I felt this dull emotional ache in the days leading up to it. Like many people, I'd grown up with by-the-numbers holiday celebrations—namely, matching red sweaters for me and my older brother, Amy Grant's Christmas CD blasting over my dad's Bose stereo system (it was the nineties!), and quiet suppers brimming with Midwestern angst. (The sound of a metal knife on a porcelain plate still makes me shudder; pass the gravy *and* the Xanax, please.)

Fast-forward past my teen years, please. At age twenty, I was cast in the *Radio City Christmas Spectacular*. With just one day off for the holiday, it was impossible to get back to Pittsburgh. Flights were prohibitively expensive. Moreover, by the time the calendar hit *actual* Christmas Eve, we'd been singing carols at the tops of our lungs since Halloween, which is when rehearsals started. I was jingle-belled out. But instead of going home, for once I was going to work, for a few hours of professional cheer.

And then Christmas morning arrived, and I got to Radio City. Every dancer in the show had brought in a casserole dish, something to pass around in the dressing rooms during the brief forty-minute breaks we'd get between shows. I remember being struck, anew, by the array of faces and backgrounds that surrounded me—how clear it was, on this holiest of days, that I was huddling up with not just Christians but also Jews and Muslims and atheist artists (hey, a gig is a gig!). And all of us were crammed between costume racks, wearing sweatpants and fake eyelashes, wolfing down such nontraditional Christmas fare as Zabar's Upper West Side chocolate babka (better than gingerbread!) and rugelach (better than sugar cookies!).

That first Christmas away from home was the exact opposite of the awkward, sit-around-the-fire affairs that had defined all my previous holidays. There wasn't a lot of lounging at Radio City. Only sweating and giggling, overeating and performing, and finally collapsing. But not a lot of kicking back—and not much crying, either. There was no time to miss home, not when we were entertaining so many tourists who were away from their own.

If you find yourself separated, voluntarily or not, from your blood relatives, try embracing and cultivating a makeshift family made of friends, coworkers, and neighbors who may be in the same boat. There are a whole bunch of us holiday orphans out there: people who, for whatever reason, fly solo or stick to the sidelines. The real holiday miracle of adulthood is that you don't always have to go back to your hometown to feel as if you're at home.

23 GO WHERE THE LOVE IS

I f it's true that everybody likes to be liked, then nobody likes to be liked more than people who literally get applause for a living. (In my writing career, it is consistently startling to not hear a group of people clapping, once I turn in a new book. The stage spoiled me.) But if a life in showbiz is largely marked by rejection, why do so many of us refuse to go where the love is? Why do we downplay the yeses and keep chasing after the *no*s?

Many of us have a hard time accepting the affection and admiration of a partner who actually wants to love us or an employer who thinks we're a fantastic hire. We either mistrust people's enthusiasm

for us or, worse, we vastly undervalue what it means to be appreciated, constantly looking over our shoulders for an even deeper high.
We think there must be something wrong with people if they think
there's something so right about us. (As in: "I only got hired for *The
Little Mermaid* because I once shared a cab with the assistant casting
director.")

Ironically, this causes a lot of us to fall into a pattern of addiction. Not to drugs, or booze. In this case, it's the lightheaded buzz of
winning over as many people as possible, as opposed to going where
the love already is—where someone is already saying, *I like you, I
want you, I need you.* We write that person off. He must be crazy. We
cast loyalty off as nepotism, and get all starry-eyed about making
the next group of people love us. And after we work ourselves into a
lather, we rinse and repeat, in perpetuity.

Loyalty isn't the lazy way out; it's often only in those comfortable, ongoing relationships that we can truly get our most dynamic
work done. Many of theater's most memorable moments were created by longtime duos. I'm talking about Donna McKechnie and
Michael Bennett, who collaborated on Cassie's iconic dance in *A
Chorus Line* after years of dancing together in other shows. In fact,
the muse list goes on and on, from Bob Fosse creating *Sweet Charity*
on Gwen Verdon to *Crazy for You* creators Susan Stroman and Mike
Ockrent. Heck, Tommy Kail and Lin-Manuel Miranda went to
the same college years before they joined forces to make Alexander
Hamilton sing.

And loyalty isn't restricted to especially lucky or talented pairs.

Open any *Playbill*, flip to the ensembles' bios, and you'll undoubtedly notice that many of them have danced for one particular choreographer—who has likely, over time, built a stable of reliable dancers he likes to rehire. There's a reason for that.

When the room is full of people who are willing to wade into murky, uncharted waters with a true spirit of trust, half the job is already done. Believe me, there is nothing quite so scary as teaching a group of dancers a new step, and hoping they don't cross their arms and judge you. Same goes with handing over a script to a group of actors for a first read-through. No matter how "high up" you get, you wanna be liked. For the kids to think your jokes are funny.

When the same actors turn up again and again, season after season, it generally means they are especially supportive of a collaborative, openhearted process that exposes the deepest desires of a creative team—who often only feel as valued as their last hit. When you go where the love is, you surround yourself with people who let you know, *You're okay. I appreciate you. We're good.* A very different motivation from: *I want to collect as many admirers as possible, even if it means ignoring the people who have stuck by my side when I was a nobody.*

Try to identify a source of love in your own life that you've consistently turned away from, or not fully embraced. You only need one big break to forever say you've been on Broadway, or one sparkling first date to lead you on the road to a solid relationship. So stop chasing after the guy who never texts you back. Sometimes hard-to-get is just too hard to live with.

24 RECOGNIZE THAT LIFE IS LIKE A MUSICAL

ooks, movies, TV shows: Each is an art form that captures a moment in as close to a "forever" way as possible, with their endless reprints and reboots and reruns. The opposite is true about the theater: You had to be there. The performances disappear the minute the curtain comes down. It becomes a memory. It's magical and a little sad.

My favorite brand of theater is summer stock, that great old tradition where you pack your bags and head to a barn (sometimes literally) of a theater, in order to put on six shows in six weeks. Now, nobody is the right "type" for every one of these musicals—the youthful gangs of *West Side Story* don't have a lot of overlap with the aging chorines of *Follies*. And thus, you're almost always miscast for about half the summer, playing roles written for people thirty years older than you.

It's the best.

It's exhausting and exhilarating. During daylight hours you're learning *42nd Street* (even though you've never tapped a day in your life) and at night you're performing *Man of La Mancha* (with a mustache that's painted on with eyeliner). Beyond the frenetic fun, what makes summer stock so lovely is simply that there's no time to get sick of anybody. You can't get bored with the job, because you've barely learned the job before the musical closes, and then it's on to the next one. Another openin', another show, and life goes on.

Every summer for three years in my teens I went to Morgantown, West Virginia—as unlikely a place as anywhere for live theater to flourish—in order to perform in half a dozen musicals at the West Virginia Public Theater. It was a trip. I stayed in a dorm room that had no air-conditioning. Sometimes, our little troupe would perform to half-full houses, who'd cross their arms during risqué bits of shows like *Cabaret*. It was West Virginia, but it was heaven. It was the joy and rush of teaming up with a disparate group of strangers to accomplish something tangible. And then, like clockwork every year, five weeks would zip by and the tent would come down. And if it weren't for the photos and the occasional group text messages, it's like it didn't even happen.

Life is like a musical: here one moment, and gone the next.

Partners come and go faster than you can swipe right; or your long-awaited Caribbean vacation gets rained out; or you've finally saved up to get a great new car when, *bam*, you pull out of the lot and have a fender bender. But what the theater teaches us again and again is that it's all just a moment. You can fight it, but it isn't going to change—at the time of this book's printing, nobody has figured out how to live forever.

And as for shows, unless you're *Phantom*, your days are probably numbered, too. You're smart to take a lot of selfies in costume, and hug your cast-mates tight, and then say good-bye, and start a text-chain with your cast, and move on to the next adventure.

25 SAVE THE DRAMA

et go of the misinformed idea that great work can only be done if you're some huge diva. In my experience, the bigger the star, the more gracious she comes—and vice versa.

Name drop alert: Bernadette Peters gave every last member of the company a special gift on their birthday during the Broadway run of *Gypsy*. Talk about a star. She also frequently picked up the tab when the entire cast would go out for drinks, and she never missed providing a "bagel Sunday," on which giant platters were delivered to the theater before our last matinee of the week, courtesy of guess who. But for as generous a leading lady as she was, it's what Bernadette *didn't* do that left the deepest impressions. She never threw a tantrum. She never talked down to the actors who weren't celebrities (read: every other member of the company). And she never even blinked when Sam Mendes, our celebrated and slightly brash British director, gave Bernadette notes in front of the entire company—a rarity in the annals of backstage etiquette. Generally, a star receives her "feedback" in the privacy of her own decked-out dressing room, but not Bernadette. She's the kind of diva who got there the old-fashioned way: through hustle and humility. *If you've got a note that'll make my performance better, give it to me. I don't care who hears.*

I swear, I learned more watching Sam give Bernadette notes on how to play a particular scene than I would have had I received the notes myself. And I only had that opportunity because Bernadette was only a diva onstage, and a dyed-in-the-wool trouper the rest of the time.

Audra McDonald, Brian d'Arcy James, Gwen Verdon, Marin Mazzie, Brian Stokes Mitchell—these might not be household names in Branson or Biloxi, but on Broadway they're our A-listers. And every last one of them is known for his or her warmth and wit. Word gets around fast. Even the positive stuff.

Maybe this notion that to command respect you've got to be some kind of demanding monster backstage is a leftover concept from the Golden Age of Hollywood, of all places—specifically those campy films that document an over-the-top take on showbiz. Look, we all giggle over *All About Eve*, with its scheming understudies and wildly histrionic actresses. Fictional stories featuring crazed lunatics are fun to enjoy with popcorn and a Coke. But movies aren't real life.

The truth is that the really gifted performers—the ones who are in it for the long haul—are nearly always all about the work. They save the drama for the stage.

Do you see this over-the-top behavior in your own life? Do you work with some of these folks who suck up all the air in the room, constantly make outrageous demands of the boss (or the employees), and generally make life unpleasant for everybody around them because of their addiction to control? Yeah, don't be that. Don't be the diva. Be the hardworking, workaday costar who chugs along merrily—and ends up with an actual, long-lasting career. He's the guy people want to have nearby on the eighth show of the week, when the whole team is exhausted. When you've gotta push through and give 'em one hell of a performance, you want to be buoyed by folks who know that work ethic trumps stupid demands. And if all that sounds like more of a leader than a follower, maybe it's because you're meant to lead, yourself. Consider this your invitation to step right up. The world is always ready for another trailblazing team player.

When you start bringing your attitude-free A-game, the only demanding thing about you will be how badly people want you around.

26 STOP SAYING YOU'RE TIRED

Pop quiz: What's the first thing you say when people ask how you are? Odds are it's some version of "Exhausted!" And they probably say, "Same." And neither of you is wrong, exactly.

It's hard work adulting, just as it's hard work being a full-time performer. Half the gig is finding a gig, the other half is staying healthy enough to go to work every day—and, since theater people suck at math, the *other* other half is staying brave, amid the demoralizing odds of making a living in showbiz. I could use a nap just thinking about it.

To create anything that matters in a world of oversaturated

media is, in itself, a fearless act, and fearlessness takes its toll. Add to that headache a pile of bills to pay, a few cats to feed and/or give special medicine twice a day, children to pick up from school and cart to soccer (except on Wednesdays, when their dad has them), and gym memberships to, in theory, actually use. It's no wonder we're all perpetually tired.

And yet, please stop saying how tired you are. Because nobody else but your partner and your therapist really cares. (And you're paying one of them.)

Legendary choreographer Martha Graham said, "There is no satisfaction whatever at any time. There is only a queer divine dissatisfaction, a blessed unrest that keeps us marching and makes us more alive than the others."

If you feel both restless and unrested, welcome to the club.

I hear it nearly every day as a default "catch up" response. "I'm tired, is how I am!" It's a sly conversation filler, because it suggests a certain street cred; exhaustion means you're running around, and running around means you're in the thick of it. Doesn't that indicate success? To some degree, sure.

But let's all, myself included, think of more novel ways of describing what we're up to. If you're zonked because you've packed your schedule with ambitious activities, that's fantastic—but no one is forcing you to hustle so hard. In fact, nobody is forcing any of us to be an artist at all. So get back to work, and when you come up for air, don't complain about it.

Is this fun advice? Nah. I don't like hearing it, either. The first

Get back to work, and when you come up for air, don't complain.

time I was told to shut up or get out was in a dance class, when I was thirteen and I'd dragged my butt into Saturday jazz. "I could still be in bed!" I remarked, not covertly, to the kid next to me, during the stretch portion of the morning. I thought I was hilarious. My fearsome teacher did not.

"I could still be in bed, too, Tim," she said, "so either leave my class or get your head in the game." My face went hot, but I'm grateful for that teacher, now. We all need someone to slap some sense into us now and then. We could use the occasional reminder that there's nothing all that captivating about the fact that you're running weary.

Am I still guilty of mindless complaints? All the time. My default reply to my boyfriend's casual "How was your day?" is a version of "It wore me out. Can we open some wine?" Which isn't exactly a turn-on, I've been told. But I've found that the most aggressively curious people I know take a certain amount of tiredness as a given. To have chosen to be a writer and a New Yorker and a tough self-critic is also to constantly be hunting for a story.

There's a certain delicious disappointment in never quite hitting the mark you aimed for. I look back at photos of myself from my dancing days and think, *How did I ever have time for auditions when I was so busy taking tap class?* I read my early writing and wonder how I ever got published. But I wouldn't trade any of these years, or experiences. They wore me out as they built me up.

Is it tough to get a good night's sleep when you've got a killer drive? Yes. But if you can tap into the resource that keeps you up past your own curfew, and can harness the thing that haunts you and use it as a secret power, you're onto something. You might be tuckered out, but you'll also be tuned in, to your true purpose. It is tiring and maddening, but also motivating.

So start asking yourself, "How am I doing?" And then don't pause when you answer, "I have a lot going on. Which is great." Because it is.

27 CLAP LOUDEST FOR THE UNDERSTUDIES

Get in the habit of making a super big deal when somebody from the shadows steps in to save the day. Take it from me: You don't want to roll your eyes when the understudy goes on.

Actually, don't take it from me—take it from seventeen-year-old me. That's how old I was when a new Broadway show opened called *Side Show*. It contained a rafter-rattling score by the writers of *Dreamgirls*, but *Side Show* was best known for its breakout star performances. Alice Ripley and Emily Skinner played blonde conjoined twins in the gothic and twisted tale, based on a true story, and I wore out their duets on the CD in my childhood bedroom. (And I wore out my brother, too, by blasting it.) I had to see this show, and I especially had to hear these ladies.

Over Christmas break my junior year of high school, I sped nine hours through a snowstorm with a friend from Pittsburgh to get to the Richard Rodgers Theatre on 46th Street in New York in time for the matinee. (Worth it!) I'd spent the entire road trip belting out the songs until I had a glorious, sore throat! I was practically hoarse in my Emily Skinner impression! But when we walked into the performance, we learned that Emily Skinner was out sick that day—and thus her understudy was on. Tragedy.

I was a teenage gay boy who knew *Side Show* so well I could have probably gone on and played the role myself that day, so I was perhaps understandably disappointed. But, crammed into the theater lobby in my Eddie Bauer winter coat and a matching Midwestern scowl, I thought nothing of declaring, and loudly: "You've got to be kidding me—Emily Skinner isn't on?"

"Her understudy is wonderful," said a lady in front of us, and my travel companion said, "What are you, the understudy's mother?" And the lady said, "Yes, I am."

(Cue: crickets.)

And guess what? The understudy wasn't just wonderful; she was sensational. A young Broadway star in her own right, named Lauren Kennedy. She landed the big punch lines, she made me weep, and, at the curtain call, Alice Ripley asked the audience to sit down so she could tell us how wonderful Lauren had been, stepping in, off and on throughout the entire two-and-a-half-month run of the show—a

Notice the little guys who step up at a moment's notice.

special point to make, as *Side Show* was technically a flop, and its closing night was the very next day. When you're playing a conjoined twin, you need a really good partner in crime to step in, and Lauren had been that to Alice, each and every time she was required to save the day. It wasn't a disappointment to see Emily's understudy; it was an honor.

I would grow up to become an understudy myself in every Broadway show I appeared in. There's a hilarious and humbling phenomenon that occurs when you're "on" for a part that's not usually yours: You exit the stage door after the show, greet three disappointed "fans," and then discover that the sidewalk outside the theater is littered with those tiny, loose understudy "insert" slips. You know, the ones that tell the audience: Sorry, you're seeing the stringer. I once walked out of an understudy performance of *Chitty Chitty Bang Bang* and nearly stepped directly on top of my own stupid, smiling face, which had been marred by somebody's boot mark. By that point, I'd grown up enough to grin at the cosmic joke of it all: Some other Midwestern gay boy had probably shown up to see our show that day and cried, "Who the hell is Tim Federle?" And hopefully I surprised him in the right way.

In your own life, notice the little guys who work double duty, and are always ready at a moment's notice to step up and work double time to cover for anyone who doesn't come through—or who *does* show up and isn't prepared, or fumbles and needs an unexpected extra hand. These team players are the MVPs of every organization.

Clap loudest for the understudies. Not only will you see a lot of them over time, but you might just be the "understudy" yourself someday. I hope when the time comes for you to step into the spotlight, you also receive the longest ovation.

28 GIVE COMPLIMENT SANDWICHES

For many of us, the only thing more difficult than receiving criticism is giving it. There's an art to providing a note, which is why the "compliment sandwich"—perfected backstage at many a Broadway show—works so well on anyone with a tendency to get prickly, any time you try to float ways in which they could improve.

So what is the compliment sandwich? You lead with something positive, then you give the note, and then you end on something good. Something nice. That's it. No calories, no mess.

I was still in my mid-twenties when I dance-captained the original company of *White Christmas* in San Francisco. That meant I had a leadership position that hovered somewhat above the chorus, many of whom were quite a bit more experienced (read: older) than I was, and all of whom I was expected to give performance notes and feedback to following our nightly shows. Before we'd even begun rehearsals, I was stressed to learn that the great and mighty Caitlin Carter had been cast in a featured role. Caitlin's got legs from her toes to her nose; for a long time you couldn't go anywhere in New York without seeing all twenty feet of her plastered on the side of a bus. She was one of the faces of the megahit *Chicago* revival—and its original dance captain. So when little old me had to tiptoe into her *White Christmas* dressing room to mention the tiniest of tweaks—like an onstage spacing issue, or to review a tap step that had gone slightly awry—I used to say to myself, like a mantra, "Lead with a compliment." My legs trembled and I could barely speak above a tight whisper, but Caitlin could not have been a more gracious note-taker—having given out so many herself.

I learned that I always felt most confident when I could stride up to Caitlin and (truthfully) start with something like: "I overheard a patron in the lobby last night talking about how gorgeous the lady in pink was in the opening number" (that was Caitlin), and then I'd dole out the smallest adjustment, like, "Check how high you're kicking in 'Blue Skies'; it should just be to your waist." And then I'd leave by saying something like, "Okay, have a fabulous matinee—I can always count on you to give 100 percent!"

And then I'd limp out to the hall and breathe into a paper bag. It ain't easy giving notes to an idol.

Yes, compliment sandwiches can be a bit time-intensive and cheesy to prepare and deliver. And true pros—including Caitlin—quickly see through the element of bullshit that surrounds it, and end up saying, "Just gimme the note." But too many people out there never quite learned that critiques are rarely personal. For them, being told how they can improve at something is an opportunity to defend their side of the story. Try not to let them. Make the notes you're giving, especially in a work environment, totally about the job at hand. Explain, calmly but unwaveringly, that explanations don't really matter to you, that you're not mad at him, that this doesn't need to be a Big Learning Moment—and that you've got other people with even bigger issues you've got to get to.

Then say something nice and get out of there.

Oh and a special note on "giving notes" at home—especially to a significant other. Remember: If you're in a leadership position at work, the giving of feedback is a big part of the territory. At home, not so much. You should mostly be striving for equality in your partnerships, and avoid amassing a list of your partner's flaws. Put another way: Try not to be the boss of your love life so much as the co-producer of your relationship.

Wherever you do try the compliment sandwich technique, remember it only works if you actually mean the authentic stuff. Be tough, but be real.

29 FOLLOW YOUR WHIMS

Follow your dreams, sure. But also—jeez, dreams are a lot of pressure, right? And the most daring dreams of all require the approximate care and upkeep of a newborn baby. Forever.

You likely grew up with various well-meaning adults pinching your cheeks and asking, "What do you want to be when you grow up?" It's worse than ever for today's young generation. In the old days, a regular kid wanted to be a basketball player. Now he wants to be a *famous* basketball player. Everybody nowadays wants to be famous for something, even if they don't know for *what*—but here's a little insight into the following of dreams. You've got to also follow your whims. Those tiny insights that aren't yet fully formed ideas.

Every person with stars in her eyes also needs a little fairy dust

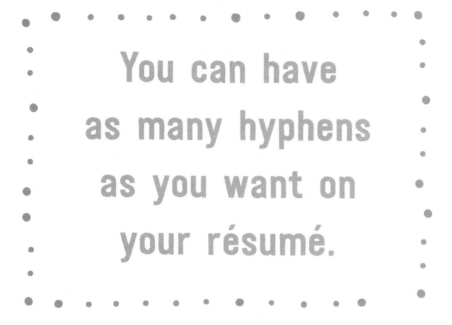

You can have as many hyphens as you want on your résumé.

in her pockets. A little something that's in the "maybe" category—a hunch, a project to carve away at slowly over time until it reveals its own shape. Or doesn't, in which case you toss it aside and move along, no tears shed.

You see, the big goals—becoming a doctor, or moving to a faraway city after a long lifetime in the same town—take a huge amount of focus and mental ambition. My own dream career was rather generic, looking back on it now. It contained all the hallmarks of a youthful yearning, because "I wanna be on Broadway!" was both incredibly vague and also extraordinarily ambitious. Sure, it meant getting from Pittsburgh to New York, and I wanted it before I was old enough to rent a car. But the problem with a plan so gigantic but also limited in scope is that, once I got it, nobody was there to tap me on the shoulder and say, "So now what?" Unfortunately, guidance counselors don't follow you into adulthood. That's why it's so important to work away at other things on the side—hobbies or secrets or something just for yourself. Your whims. The things that don't feel they'll add up to much, or seem like they could be unlikely hits.

Theater history is full of folks who futzed around on side projects on their way to the big time. Lin-Manuel Miranda created *Hamilton* after reading an Alexander Hamilton biography on vacation from *In the Heights*. Talk about whimsical: a multicultural hip-hop retelling of a historical figure's life story? It'd never work on paper—now you can't get a ticket.

Meredith Willson was just a bandleader who toiled away for ten thankless years on a venture that would become *The Music Man*. Mitch Leigh wrote throwaway jingles before tilting at windmills with his own breakthrough *Man of La Mancha*. Heck, Sherman Edwards of *1776* fame was a high school history teacher until his musical about the Declaration of Independence debuted to acclaim.

The polite thing for these writers to have pursued—the version of life that would have disrupted *nobody*—would have essentially been doing what they'd always done, like grading papers at night instead of secretly hammering out songs. But they followed their hunches instead. They changed the world with their whims.

I spent most of my twenties feeling pretty voiceless, as a performer who sometimes appeared wearing oversize animal costumes—like when I was a dancing polar bear at Radio City. It took me ages to realize that all my journal entries and long-winded emails spoke to something true about a more fully fledged me: that I could be a dancing polar bear *and* have a voice. That you don't have to choose. That you can have as many hyphens as you'd like on your résumé.

Throughout my life, the thing that came even more naturally to me than dancing around was joking around. When I at last became a "real writer," I took the hobby that got me in trouble my whole life (being a goof-off) and turned it into my primary source of income— and satisfaction (having "a voice"!). But this new life started as a small action. A blog post. A tweet. A diary entry that became the first chapter of a secret book I was writing for nobody but myself. It was a whim before it was a reality. Frogs start as tadpoles. Or, more aptly, polar bears start as cubs.

In the storage area in the back of your brain, where you keep those pie-in-the-sky fantasies, make sure to leave room for a couple of barely detectable shooting stars. The pottery class, or the French lessons, or the hours you spend collecting driftwood and making funky art that you've never shown anyone. Sometimes these whims will pay off—even if the only thing they make richer is your own self-image.

30 RECOVER BETWEEN PERFORMANCES

Every performer knows that you have to take time to take care of yourself. (There's a reason I stopped dancing at age twenty-eight, and it involves the realization that painkillers had become a nightly snack.) Not enough of us build self-care into our daily lives, and that's a mistake, because we give our best performances when we've recovered.

Take a tour of any backstage theater dressing room and you could be mistaken for thinking it's a gym. Yoga mats are strewn everywhere, along with therapy bands, plastic steaming masks, and handwritten signs with arrows pointing to physical therapy. Truly grueling, dance-heavy shows even have massage therapists on-site—but it ain't a spa. Honestly, one of the biggest ongoing challenges of any long-running show is just bending over to change your damn costume-shoes ten times a night (seriously)—not to mention climbing up six flights of stairs for a five-minute breather in your dressing room. These are old buildings. They don't have elevators. They have cockroaches and cranky doormen and clanking pipes, and to counterbalance those stresses, you have to take the time to decompress.

I read that Cynthia Erivo, the powerhouse star of *The Color Purple* revival, drank shots of ginger in between performances. (Go YouTube Ms. Erivo wailing "I'm Here" through the roof, and you'll see that the ginger paid off.) Hey, whatever works. There's a degree of superstition when your body is your job. But, in a way, aren't all of us in debt to our bodies?

I personally never felt older than I did when I was twenty. Lemme explain. The Radio City stage is made of steel—unlike most stage decks, which are constructed of wood, a natural material that "gives" a bit when you land, hard, from a jump. But at twenty, I was clomping, stomping, and sometimes limping across Radio City's brutal metal deck, built that way to support sophisticated stage hydraulics and lifts. The versatility of the Radio City stage made for a visually dynamic show, but try telling that to my knees.

One of the older dancers back then gave me a valuable tip: If I wanted to survive the season, I was going to have to take nightly ice baths—which is exactly as awful as it sounds. You come home, dump a pound of ice into a bathtub (during the winter, on the East Coast),

Counteract some of your mental aches and scrapes.

and then . . . well, there are different techniques. There's the "jump in and temporarily hate your life" technique, or the "slowly ease in and hate all of the choices that led to this moment" version. Either way, you submerge your throbbing bones into the ice water, and stay put as long as you can. Wine helps. So does Advil. (I'm no doctor, so technically I'm not prescribing wine *and* Advil at once.) Sometimes you'd cry—but you'd cry harder the next day if you hadn't taken that bath to reduce inflammation.

Isn't showbiz glamorous?

So, okay, your day-to-day life probably doesn't involve jumping up and down for four thousand screaming children while wearing a polar bear costume—and by the way, congrats if it doesn't. But you've still got stressors, both physical and mental. I know you do. And if you don't counteract some of those aches, scrapes, and shouts, you're adding a lot of mental plaque to your overall health score. So make a list of all the crap you put up with—the morning subway commute, the loudmouth coworker in the open-plan office, the way you no longer sleep soundly if you've had coffee after 3 p.m. And now think up some way you could counteract those things—kind of like offsetting your carbon footprint, but emotionally.

Does it mean budgeting in a day at the gym just for yoga, so you aren't always only pumping iron? You can't give it your all if you don't have a lot to give. Does this mean taking another five minutes in the morning to download your favorite podcast, so you're starting the day in the frame of mind you need for peak performance, and aren't walking out the door in reactive mode? My life changed the day I started waking up fifteen minutes *earlier*, despite feeling tired at first. Suddenly I had a moment to get ahead of the day, instead of chasing after it to keep up.

Find ways to reset and recharge. A performance of a lifetime is made up of how you spend your time. Your audience deserves to feel taken care of, and so do you.

31 RECRUIT A FRIEND TO ASSESS YOUR AUDITION OUTFIT

First impressions matter, sure, but to make an impact, you don't need to appear as if you've, like, leapt off the pages of *Vogue*. You just need to *feel* as if you have.

One of my very first auditions in New York City was for a Super Bowl halftime show. (Halftime shows are like intermissions for straight people.) I was young. I was not savvy. I had no wardrobe budget. But I'd taken a ten-hour bus ride from Pittsburgh to show off my stuff, and I wore to this audition my "signature outfit" at the time—black, flair-legged tights, high-top sneakers, and a green polo shirt. As in: a collared cotton jersey knit, the type you'd wear to a picnic on a brutally hot day, except instead I wore it to every single dance audition. Nearly all the other guys, savvy New Yorkers, showed off their quadlike biceps in black tank tops (always black). But not me, and for good reason: My arms were toothpicks. I looked terrible in a tank top, like a malnourished philosophy major. And thus, I felt like my most comfortable self in that green polo shirt—and dammit, when you feel comfortable, you feel great. And when you feel great, you actually look great—or can trick the world into thinking you do.

The reason I'd settled on a green polo shirt in the first place is that an older, more experienced dancer back home had advised me that I'd "stand out" (ha!) if I wore a shirt that highlighted my "all-American boyish youth." And guess what? I ended up dancing behind Christina Aguilera at that damn Super Bowl, even though I showed up to the audition looking like I'd raided a Gap Kids in the dark.

(Still have no idea which teams actually played in that particular game, so please don't ask. The year was 2000. Phil Collins also appeared in the halftime show, as did Toni Braxton and, for reasons I'll never understand, noted actor Edward James Olmos. When you find the YouTube video, do not share it online.)

Back to fashion. Recruit a friend who has style to spare. You know the one. He (because it's almost always a *he*) is the "fashion guy," whose Instagram account could be acquired by the Museum of Modern Art. Invite him over. Have him assess your latest dating profile pic, and methodically explain why this particular selfie angle doesn't work (or does!). Guide the conversation so he doesn't wither you with his comments, but rather he empowers you.

Ultimately, you want to blow people away with your persona, not your pantsuit. But in a world that overvalues looks, you might as well show up with the best-feeling package you've got. It'll knock their socks off.

32 ARRIVE A HALF HOUR BEFORE HALF HOUR

I f you want to get ahead, get to work first. Showing up ahead of schedule isn't simply about your job, though. Whether it's gearing up for a date or getting into the mind-set for a big interview, warming up physically and mentally is about putting on your best face, and getting flexible for whatever might happen.

I was lucky enough to work on the West End of London some years ago. There's a tradition of "warming up for the show" that's actually built into the regular schedule. An hour before the show, the entire cast—from the chorus boys to the leading lady—gathers onstage for a group warm-up. It's humbling, because everyone looks a bit crazed. The ladies stand around in wig-caps, their faces half made-up. The boys wear frumpy sweatpants and a lot of blush. Nobody is quite ready for an audience, and everyone's on their phones, and there's a lot of chitchat and catching up before the dance captain leads a group stretch. But gathering early, on automatic and with intention, is about more than socializing. First, it's just plain smart, because warm-ups have been shown to reduce injury. A mandatory group warm-up also gives the show's music conductor a chance to tell thirty people, at once, that their diction is getting a bit sloppy in the big Act Two dance number. Otherwise, he's chasing people down or tacking notes to a corkboard. In London, where everyone congregates onstage before the show, you don't have to worry about mixed messaging. You just say it right to the person, like as in the old days.

Not so in the States. In American theater, for whatever reason, actors are simply required to appear a half hour before curtain. Whether they warm up or not is all on them. Since arriving home from the UK, I've come to find this a bit nuts; so many pulled hamstrings could be avoided! And so much miscommunication could be eliminated, too, if people were required to, ya know, *communicate*, face-to-face. Instead, the backstage creative staff on Broadway run around leaving little Post-it notes on performers' dressing room tables, hoping actors correctly interpret a scribbled note about their performance.

Getting to work early and gathering at the water cooler with your coworkers doesn't just reduce the kind of agitation that nobody likes—it also feeds a culture of togetherness. Now, I'm not suggesting that you and thirty cubicle-mates get to the break room a half hour early to stand in a circle and hum a friggin' folk song—but I am saying there is wisdom in intentional focus. In pushing for a group mind-set that says: Let's attack this big ol' thing as a team. In taking the time to take the time.

It's worth noting that warming up doesn't have to be arduous. People hear *warm-up* and they think *gym* and when they think *gym* they think: *I'd rather be on the sofa watching* The Bachelor. (Me too, by the way.) Warming up can and should be something simple that gets your butt into the building. Like sitting at your desk while it's still quiet, and rewarding yourself with a second cup of coffee. Whatever works for you.

To prepare for her title role in *The Little Mermaid* every night, Sierra Boggess used to blast Barbra Streisand albums, and belt along with the high notes, all while the hair and makeup teams fluttered around her. Sometimes I'd poke my head in on the way to my own dressing room, several floors up, and not even say anything. I'd just smile at a pro getting ready to wow the masses, one warm-up at a time.

33 IMAGINE YOUR HERO IN THE AUDIENCE

Wherever you are, in whatever job you're doing, you're going to face sleepy "matinee" days when you'd rather be anywhere but your cubicle—and you've got to trick yourself into giving the gig your all. I'm not talking about washing the dishes or cleaning out your glove compartment. Feel free to phone those performances in. I'm talking about the realities of the big time. The flip side of a dream job is that it's still a job. Welcome to the real world—now prepare to sweat.

When I was a coach for *Billy Elliot* on Broadway, the child actors and I would occasionally talk about all the varied ways one can

Muses work in mysterious ways.

motivate oneself to give a full-out performance. Again and again, I returned to one trick with the boys: I'd ask them, "Who's your favorite singer?" or "Who's your all-time favorite dancer?" Maybe they'd say Taylor Swift, or Mikhail Baryshnikov—and now I had something to work with. We'd make a game out of imagining what would happen if they gave a performance as Billy, and immediately following the curtain call they walked out the stage door and *bam!* There was Taylor or Mikhail, holding out a *Playbill* for them to sign. "Would you be delighted," I'd ask the boys, "because you'd left your heart and soul on the stage in a pool of sweat, and your all-time favorite hero was there to witness it?" Alternatively, "Would you feel mortified, like you wanted a do-over, because you'd assessed the audience as half-interested and thus gave them half a performance?"

There are all sorts of compelling and tempting reasons not to give something your all: sleepiness, laziness, more fun to let your mind wander. Hard work is hard work. I'd ultimately issue the boys a challenge: "On performance day, it's one or the other: you'll either go for it, or you'll leave your passion in the dressing room, along with your Power Bar and Gatorade." And it worked. They'd put their favorite person in the back row of the theater, and they'd do the show for her. It gave the performance a specific drive, and a purpose: You're not entertaining twelve hundred generic audience members. You're trying to impress your hero.

I should note that I did not think up this "hero game" myself. When Tommy Tune danced in *My One and Only* on Broadway, he is said to have imagined the famed "water dancer" Esther Williams out in the audience, particularly during the number when he had to splash around in puddles while sporting tap shoes. (Ah, showbiz.)

When you're running low on motivation, imagine the person *you* most admire, out there in the "audience"—or over your shoulder, watching you navigate through tricky or just plain grueling work. By choosing a hero—and it doesn't have to be a celebrity; choose the college professor you most admired, if you'd like—you're getting at the core of why so many of us do what we do: because we desire to be seen. How many jobs (or marriages) end because one of you begins to feel invisible?

Figure out who your Esther Williams, Taylor Swift, or Mikhail Baryshnikov is, and the next time an important task feels like a slog, put that person in the room with you. Impress them. Delight them. Surprise them, even if they are your only witness. Muses work in mysterious ways. Just make them work for you.

34 REHEARSE UNDER EMERGENCY CONDITIONS

Too many of us go through life getting easily thrown off course by unexpected changes in our environment. Racing to work, you hit a wall of traffic and your mood is a solid zero for the whole day. Or, in the middle of a high-stakes presentation, the microphone goes out and it flusters you. You never recover. Truly elite performers learn to rehearse for mistakes, because something goes wonky in nearly every live performance. It's what you do when the skit hits the fan that defines your professionalism.

Midway through my stint as one of the kids' tap-dance coaches on *Billy Elliot*, I'd grown frustrated with a recurring phenomenon. Our otherwise brilliant child actors, whom we'd trained for months on end in a rehearsal studio, would finally have their chance to practice onstage before making their big debuts—and one by one they each fell apart. "The stage is too slippery," they'd say, or the lights were too blinding, or the music was way faster than the CD we'd been rehearsing with. It drove me batty, though I couldn't blame them. *Billy Elliot* is such a wildly demanding show—requiring a British accent, crazy ballet turns, the ability to sing in a clarion soprano *and* do a time step *and* cry on cue, all at age twelve—that it would take a huge team of people the better part of half a year to prep each kid to make his debut. But time and again, no matter how talented the boys were, when we'd bring each of them from the rehearsal studio to the stage, they had a mini freak-out. It slowed us down and eroded the boys' confidence.

On one of my days off from the show, I was flipping through channels when I came upon an interview with the swimmer Michael Phelps. (I don't typically watch sports, but, ya know, his abs.) Phelps was being grilled about one particular swim meet, where he'd set a world record and won a gold medal—even though one of the lenses of his goggles had accidentally filled with water after he dove into the pool. That is, he'd swum half-blind and *still* won. So how did he do it? Without missing a beat, Phelps said, "Because my coach made me practice it that way."

Aha! Phelps regularly swam under emergency conditions—with the lights off under the pool, with rock music blaring at times, and with one goggle full of water. Only one day or so per week was spent rehearsing (whoops, practicing) as if everything was going to go right once he got underwater. On game day, I learned, you've gotta prep your athlete for anything—and this was a revelation to me as a coach.

I started rehearsing with the Billys differently, following that rare stop at ESPN. Now our artistic staff would leave the rehearsal floor slippery sometimes; or we'd instruct the boys to face away from the mirrors while dancing to "throw them off"; or we'd have them try pirouetting with their eyes closed . . . with the lights flashing . . . with the piano player going wayyyy toooo slowwwwly or wy too fst! And it worked. The boys started adapting to the reality that, in a live performance, they wouldn't feel the comfortable safety net of an artificial rehearsal environment. It would be faster, slipperier, scarier, slower, louder, and different. And ultimately, more exciting, and "live."

Build a backup plan into any critical element of your day that could go wrong. The genius of GPS is that it can automatically recalculate the fastest route to your destination. Get in the habit of bulking up your internal map so you don't flinch so hard when your deck crashes on the day of the big pitch. Wing it, using a well-devised Plan B.

Too many of us only go through the paces under perfection conditions—we "can't" take the big test unless we have utter silence, and the room is seventy degrees, and our pencil is sharpened just the way we like it. Whenever possible, throw that stuff out. The ability to make do with what you've got means you're as nimble as a stage performer, able to push through even when the sound goes out, the lights go off, and the audience holds its breath to see how you'll pull through.

35 WRITE FAN LETTERS

For a lot of folks, expressing all the colorful ways in which you think something sucked is shorthand for *I have distinctive and excellent taste*. But calling out misfires, artistic and otherwise, is for amateurs. The real pros grow more sensitive over time to just how difficult brilliant work is to achieve. Once you've attempted to make your own thing—and frankly, after you've missed the mark once or twice—your respect for the true masters deepens. You stop noticing what sucks and start seeing what succeeds.

When I was interviewing script assistants for *Tuck Everlasting*, I'd always break the ice by asking people what their favorite recent musical was. Easy enough, right? But I was struck by how many applicants led off by naming five shows they'd *hated*, productions they thought had fallen flat on Broadway—which they'd name and then punctuate with an eye roll, like we were in on a big joke. Except we weren't. In fact, that's the moment they lost the job.

This is something a lot of younger folks, especially, do: expressing distaste for something as a way of showing they've got critical chops. And yet the types of people who create and foster the most ambitious work—not to mention healthy relationships, in general—are the ones who never quite lose the attitude of being fans themselves.

So write a fan letter. Today. No, really—like, not metaphorically. Maybe once a week, or even just once a month, set aside a scheduled five minutes to jot a note to someone, letting her know how great you think she is. Make it specific.

Write an email to your old guidance counselor, to let her know how much it meant to you that she had your back when you were a flailing teen. (Not enough educators get the shout-outs they deserve.) Pull your partner aside or even just send him a text in the middle of the day, mentioning one thing about him that inspires you, or gets you revved up. Try to populate your life with the types of costars who feed on positive reinforcement, and not snark. Snark is fun for, like, ten minutes, in the corner of a holiday party that you'd rather not be at. But over the long haul it grows stale. Snark has an expiration date, and once you open that can it goes bad, fast. Fandom is forever.

These letters don't have to be a huge commitment. They don't even have to be letters. It could be a one-line email dashed off to a long-ago classmate, taking special note of an accomplishment he's posted on Facebook, a message that goes beyond a Like. The point is to get into the habit of noticing when people do something you admire—and then telling them.

Think of somebody whose efforts make your life better or function more easily. It could be your dog walker or a babysitter or that neighbor who waters your plants when you're out of town. Next time she helps you out, text her: *Appreciate you, mean it.* Which is what it all boils down to anyway: *Because you're around, my existence is better.* That's it. Send.

Never get so big that you stop admiring the efforts of others. Sometimes the people who make it look the easiest are the ones working the most doggedly, and not with a whole lot of recognition from the types of people *they* might consider heroes. One of them might be you.

36 BE NICE OUTSIDE THE AUDITION ROOM, TOO

What would happen if you began treating every moment of your life as if it were an audition? Okay, maybe not *every* moment—laundry day is allowed to just be laundry day. But there's wisdom to remembering that we're all being evaluated constantly. Sure, most of us, when we walk into a first date or a job interview or, hell, a Halloween party, have been thoughtful enough to wear a clean shirt, spritz a little cologne, and generally put our friendliest foot forward. That's not telling a lie or being fake—it's taking an internal tally of your strengths and choosing those particularly shiny qualities to showcase to the public, that is, the world. This is natural. When we're under a spotlight, we behave a certain way—but it's what happens afterward, when you think nobody's watching, that defines your true character. You've gotta be nice outside the audition room, too, even when it doesn't go the way you wish it had.

Being gossipy with anyone other than your closest buds is kind of dumb from a pragmatic perspective. Word travels fast, especially in the arts, about the types of folks who are unkind and ungracious on a karmic level. Anyone can be cool in the audition room, when all eyes are clearly on them. It's how you act directly after a high-stakes situation—like, when you step into the hallway after receiving a clench-smiled "That's all we need to see today, thanks"—that speaks real volumes. Don't punch the wall. Take a deep breath and duck out onto the street instead.

I'm not talking about not confiding in your bestie when the going gets really rough. We've all called our friends and shouted into the phone about somebody else getting a gig (or boyfriend) we thought we were perfect for. (There's a time and place for that kind of unfiltered downloading—usually 11 p.m. on a Friday with a pint of Ben and Jerry's Chunky Monkey open on your lap.) I'm talking about the day-to-day persona you're putting out into the world—especially when you're broadcasting your hot takes online. Think about what kind of person you'd want to hire if you were in charge.

The bosses of today are, I guarantee you, googling everyone in their orbit—from former employees to potential applicants. I can't tell you the number of times I've sat behind a big table, at the end of a long day of casting, with a group of ten to twenty "final" actors'

Think about the
day-to-day
persona you're
putting out into
the world.

headshots spread out in front of the bleary-eyed creative team. Frequently, you're only looking for, say, five or six people to cast, so you have to start making difficult decisions. Difficult because, generally speaking, every person whose photo is on the table is talented enough to have made it to "the end." They've all got Broadway credits, really good teeth, and top agents. So how do you choose? How do you cut the group down by half, or more, when top-level talent becomes relatively interchangeable? Invariably, someone on the creative team will pipe up to say that so-and-so was trouble on another show—lazy, or uncooperative, or not great about taking notes—and just like that, he's off the table. Literally. You move on to somebody else. A better team player. Maybe candidate B won't be quite as vivid as candidate A, but vivid wears off quickly when you're stuck with a jerk in a dressing room for eight shows a week. You hire the nice guy. Nice doesn't go out of style. Nice goes with everything. Nice is the little black dress of adulthood.

Always remember that the world is a small place with a huge number of gifted people. If it comes down to you and one other person, don't lose out on an opportunity that you'd otherwise be ideally suited for, just because you weren't thoughtful when you left the room after a disappointing audition, interview, or even date. (Basically, if it's a high-pressure situation, in which you're trying to impress somebody else, it counts here.)

No matter what happens, walk to the elevator, count backwards from ten, and wait till you hit the street before you call your therapist to complain about how crazy the world is for not recognizing your outstanding skill set. Even if you're right, the casting director's assistant may be riding the elevator down with you. Save any and all outbursts for the street, lest she run back upstairs to tell the team that they dodged a bullet in letting you go. Life is short, but people's memories are long.

37 KEEP A PHOTO OF THE WORST GIG YOU EVER HAD

Try to maintain the perspective that no matter what your situation, it could probably be worse. Barring actual tragedy (like being thrown on for an understudy role you barely know), your list of problems would probably look mighty attractive to a whole lot of people out there. But they're still your problems—and if you're able to remind yourself that you've gotten through tough times before, your view of them might shift a bit. In fact, you might even have a laugh over them.

When I made my Broadway debut at the Shubert Theater in *Gypsy*, I kept a strange photograph on my dressing room table of a grown adult man wearing what appeared to be some kind of Halloween costume: big yellow feet with a beak to match, framed by black felt wings. Folks, that man was me—and I'm all dressed up like a bird for a three-week production of *The Wizard of Oz* that I performed in at the age of twenty-one in North Carolina. (A production that truly taught me there's no place like home.)

Why the photo? Because anytime I'd feel frustrated with current work politics, or on-the-job jealousies, or the day-to-day exhaustions of doing eight shows a week, all I had to do was flick my eyes over to that slightly surreal photo of a grown man shouting "Caw!" And then I'd instantly think: *Well, I've had it worse.*

It wasn't so much a miserable gig as an emasculating one; I was literally playing a crow. I got neck cramps, because I had to keep my face ducked down throughout the show, so that my black crow's-head baseball hat costume would be visible to the audience. And, listen, there are even worse gigs than that—at least it paid, and got me health insurance! Nonetheless, that little photo offered me a bird's-eye view of my own life every time I looked at it.

I'm on Broadway, I'd think. *I'm not playing an animal. I'm not working away from home.* I was appearing nightly as a human being in New York City and sleeping in my own bed. Things were okay.

What is that thing in your own life—the cringe-inducing moment you look back on and think, *I can't believe I was once so young or dumb or desperate to do that?* Incredibly ambitious people have an almost constantly moving target: the next bull's-eye they want to hit. But the smart ones also remember how, once upon a lifetime, they didn't have the connections or just plain wisdom that they've earned now.

Try to look back at a situation from your past that they couldn't pay you enough to repeat. And then laugh it off and get back to work.

38 DON'T REVIEW A SHOW ON-SITE

et's play Choose Your Own Adventure. But, like, Broadway-style.

You have just sat through the worst performance in memory. A ballad that was written to make you weep instead made you scream-laugh. In a bad way. And not just you—entire rows of people found themselves howling at what transpired before them, their shoulders bobbing with church laughter despite everyone's efforts to remain respectful. It was glorious. It was awful. It was gloriously awful. Perhaps the leading actor was suffering through a cold, and couldn't hit the high note, and thus you suffered through his cold, too. And yet, you didn't leave at intermission! You stayed.

For whatever reason, you stuck it out and sat through it and got to the end, even though the show never got better. And now, the house lights come up, and you look at your date—and whaddya say?

If you're like a lot of people, you get really honest (and noisy), and begin vocally reviewing the performance, probably with a bunch of theatrical arm movements thrown in to punctuate the takedown. "That. Was. Terrible."

I witness this all the time when I'm out and about at shows. It's human nature. And now I'm going to beg you not to. Not just at the theater, but anywhere that somebody has put himself out there: Resist the urge to give an immediate "review."

My friend Eric and I have a "three-block" rule. The rule is: Once you get approximately three blocks away from the theater, there ought to be enough tourists and sidewalk vendors milling around—not to mention taxi drivers leaning on their horns—for you to safely and genuinely exhale, and giggle, and express your unbridled thoughts about the performance. Especially a rough performance. But, please, only when you're three blocks away. It's too risky otherwise.

Besides being kind of cruel, when you debrief on-site, you do yourself a disservice, because people remember faces and they remember being poorly evaluated. (That leading guy with the sinus infection? His wife is sitting in front of you. She already had a tough night. Don't make it worse.) This extends to movies as well. How many times did you love an indie film only to have the lights come back up at the end, and the people behind you say, "Well, *that* was boring." Moment ruined.

In life, think about your surroundings, both off the Internet and on, before dogging something. Also, ask yourself: *Why am I dogging something at all?* Is it because I'm genuinely interested in how this seemingly promising project went so wrong? Or is to elevate my own sense of self by pointing out someone else's shortcomings?

Maybe you've seen this kind of circumstance illustrated in other ways. For instance, a colleague gives a presentation at work that goes hilariously off the rails. He opens his laptop, knocks a cup of coffee all over the keyboard, and doesn't have a backup plan. Or something worse. Jokes don't land, new ideas feel creaky, the pitch sucks. Whatever happens, I encourage you to keep your thoughts both off-line and off-site. The break room pairs well with mild gossip, but not authentically critical hit jobs.

Walk three blocks before you unload, however far that means to you. Better, ask yourself what you'd like people to be saying about you if you screwed up or missed the mark. Aim to be *that* person. And if you can be critical *and* careful, good-humored but not God-awful, you win the ultimate prize: being one of the good guys. The world can never use enough of those.

39 FORGIVE YOURSELF FOR A BAD PERFORMANCE

Don't let a bad performance tarnish an otherwise good day. In the name of humility you can edge into a weird kind of narcissism—and that goes doubly for all you perfectionists out there. A single fluke does not define you. This is a lesson I wish I'd known when I was beginning my professional career as a dancer.

I grew up a lot when I turned twenty. I was performing full time, having skipped college for a shot at the gypsy life—and I got it. Every musical theater dancer dreams of appearing in *A Chorus*

Line, the iconic Michael Bennett musical from the seventies that stars dancers as dancers, talking and crying about what it's like to go from show to show. At twenty, I packed my duffel bag and headed to St. Louis for the summer to play the role of Mark in *A Chorus Line*—notable because he's both the youngest character onstage and also one of the few people who actually gets "cast" in the fictional show within the show. That means I had to dance like hell, be a standout from moment number one, project to the audience: *Look at me dancing my ass off over here. Aren't I the best one up here?* No pressure, kid.

You can imagine my frustration when, only three minutes into our first preview, I badly botched a piece of famous choreography—a turning sequence in the show's legendary "audition scene" for which I was placed downstage, front and center, for what felt like all of Missouri to see me suck. I stumbled, fell, landed flat on my ego. It ruined my day, and very nearly the rest of the summer, this nagging suspicion that I'd been found out—that I was a faker and not truly talented. (Ah, the drama of being twenty.)

I shared all of this with my boyfriend at the time, and how humiliated I felt. He didn't blink, and instead said, "Wait till you get to Radio City; you do so many shows there's no time to worry about mistakes." And he was dead right.

The Christmas season after that summer in St. Louis, I donned ten costumes over five shows a day to entertain the masses at Rockefeller Center. And you know what? I messed up all the time, tripping over my own tired feet. But I kept dancing, and I learned to trust the *trend* of my talent—that, more often than not, I did a perfectly good show and occasionally a pretty flawless one. You only get that experience when you get a *lot* of experience, slogging it out thirty-five Christmas pageants a week. Wisdom means knowing, over the long haul, that you're pretty all right.

Forgive yourself when you screw up. Develop a sense of humor that allows you to snort-giggle before anyone else can. Find the funny in your mistakes, and then gently but seriously try to figure out if you are truly error-prone or just occasionally unlucky—which is also known as being human.

When a toddler falls, she gets right back up. When a dancer falls, we hold our breath, cross our fingers, and hope he does, too. We root for him. Whenever possible, offer yourself that same care. You're worth it.

40 PUT ON A HAPPY FACE

There's no people like show people, who smile when they are low . . . if they're being paid for it. But there's actual wisdom in forced merriment. Allow me to talk science for a moment. This will only hurt a bit.

There are studies (a lot of 'em, and they're bookmarked on my laptop because they comfort me!) confirming that you can trick your body into thinking you're in a relatively okay mood simply by putting on a happy face. There's apparently a stress-relieving chemical that's released when you grin like an idiot, whether you feel like grinning (or looking like an idiot) or not. Show-people know that, whether you're in a grin-and-share-it mind-set or not, if the number calls for a cheeseball smile, you deliver. Anytime I had to perform an upbeat tap dance, even if I clomped through it, utterly uninspired, I'd leave the stage feeling . . . pretty neutral, actually. All the beaming seemed to bounce off the audience and back at me. You might try it sometime. There are worse things than neutral some days.

This is firmly *not* about smiling for other people—or pretending "Everything's okay, I swear!" all the time. Smiling, when you'd rather be sulking, is more about doing a force-restart on the complicated

You can trick your brain into mild, temporary elation.

wiring of your own hard drive. And, hey, if you end up getting a reputation as being pretty upbeat along the way, that's cool, too.

When I was in middle school, I had a truly eccentric theater teacher named Jill (I believe she owned a different silk scarf for every day of the year), who gave me a nonfiction book about stagecraft that I devoured in one sitting. It was called *Theater of the Oppressed*, a fitting title for a teenage boy who felt the entire world was judging him. Written by famed Brazilian theater maker Augusto Boal, who staged guerrilla shows in the streets, the book contained a famous saying: "Have the courage to be happy." I needed that at fifteen. I need it now, too, sometimes.

The inertia of good luck seems to follow people who, more or less, appear to be enjoying themselves. Notice how the world around you is full of two types of costars. The ones who, just like vivid musical theater characters, believe their best days are ahead ("Maybe this time!" as the song goes)—or, alternatively, behind them ("I'm losing my mind").

Back to science. Set a timer. Smile for thirty seconds. Even if it's by yourself, with tears streaming down your face, in the dark. You can trick your brain into mild, temporary elation by putting on a happy face. The powerful thing about being a guy who generally goes with the flow and shines through life is that, when the going gets rough and you need to speak up, people take notice. It's the opposite of the boy who cried wolf. You become the boy who is so agreeable that when you say, "No, this isn't right," people listen.

Many highly regarded actors can only figure out their

performances from the outside in—they've got to put on the 1940s costume gloves to truly understand how their character breathes and feels. So why shouldn't you occasionally play the part of someone who's braver than you might actually be?

Don't put on a happy face for anybody but yourself. And, for pity's sake, certainly not for any construction worker on the street *telling* you to smile. (Just take this book and throw it at that guy's head.) But try this technique sometime during a low-grade fever of a day. And if you can't muster a grin, then write a gratitude note to somebody or force yourself to take a dance class.

Or just go with the stormy feelings, after all, and blast the *Spring Awakening* cast album so your breakdown has a soundtrack. Then wake up and try to find that happy face again tomorrow.

41 RECONNECT WITH YOUR INNER THEATER KID

Our childhoods were probably pretty different. Maybe bliss, for you, did not involve blasting the *Evita* cast album (don't call it a soundtrack) while acting out the title role, despite your not being Argentinian, or female, or a dictator. Regardless, I'm willing to bet that you had *some* activity that kept you occupied hour after hour when you were around eight years old. And I'd bet even more that you've lost touch with that thing. That spark. That obsession. Here's the good news: That "theater kid" still lives inside you—you just have to access him again.

I'm not choosing the age eight arbitrarily. There was a study done stating that the person you were in about second grade—her quirky pastimes and fantasies for the future—was a strong indicator of who you were genuinely meant to be, once you got a couple feet taller. For a lot of us, it was the age when our daydreams went from generic ("I'd like to be playing hopscotch on the playground right now") to specific ("I'd like to play Belle in *Beauty and the Beast* on Broadway before I'm twenty").

But for too many of us, these elementary school years were also a time when others started raising an eyebrow at our youthful passions. And thus, by third grade, we began living our lives for the adults around us. That's a hard habit to break—especially when you grew up getting a gold sticker for being "good," even at stuff you didn't care much for. Being good is the opposite of being brilliant. I'd rather get a red X any day.

A lot of people say they got into theater because it offered an escape, a chance to at last be somebody else. I got into the theater because it was the one place I could actually be myself, warts and wigs and all. Your own inner theater kid—whoever that kid was—is a north star back toward a place in your life where you got lost in your imagination.

What made time stand still for you? Who were you, back when no one was looking? These questions are not rhetorical. They are, in fact, a directive. A clarion call to get back in touch with an authentic part of yourself.

For me to reliably get into a "flow," it was a toss-up between staging complicated routines in my parents' basement *or* working on my childhood comic strip, which I called *The Weird Way* (my own take on *The Far Side*). At some point, I guarantee you an adult informed me I had to pick one—be a choreographer or be a cartoonist. Worse, I was probably told I should pick a more practical adult ambition (as if there's anything particularly practical about slaving away in a cubicle for forty years).

But you don't have to pick a single major in life, and your inner kid knew that from the start. Your inner kid was likely dead set on growing up to be a professional veterinarian-astronaut-lawyer-hula-hooper, back when she didn't know "better." Go back and find some of that mad scientist sparkle you had before you started editing yourself. Or, rather, before an adult taught you to sand down your most interesting edges.

Because I write theater-themed novels for children, sometimes I have the joy of popping into a school for the day as its guest author, and signing a lot of books. I like to have a dialogue with the kids, above anything else. Invariably, when I ask a class of second graders, "Who here considers themselves a writer?" every last hand pops up. It's adorable. It's true, too—second graders can spin a yarn, man. But when I'm touring with my novel for teens, and I ask the same question, basically . . . no hands go up. By senior year in high school, we've all been so beaten over the head with the supposed merits of topic sentences and the proper usage of semicolons that we've forgotten how to tell an actual story. But every second graders knows how to—they just start spouting. The more rules we pile onto ourselves, the less of a chance we have at striking true inspiration. It's hard to innovate when you're so busy being polite.

If you find yourself trying to figure out what kind of adult you should be, think back to what your younger self paid attention to. There's wisdom in who you were, back before you knew you had to be somebody.

42 TAKE THE NOTE

usicals are living organisms, whose performances change, stretch, and ... let's say "grow," from night to night, whether you want them to or not. Along with the blessing of this most immediate art form comes its own curse. Over the course of a show's (hopefully long) run, actors begin taking tremendously thoughtful if misguided pauses during soliloquies, dancers start straying from their onstage marks, and shows basically tend to grow lethargic faster than you can say "Wednesday matinee audience."

Early on I learned, the hard way, to just "take the note"—that if my dance captain tells me my energy is lagging in a production number or that I'm doing some new, weird thing with my arms, just to say thank-you and not offer an excuse or explanation. Nobody much cares, not really; they've got twenty other dancers to monitor and give notes to on any given night.

But when I first began receiving performance feedback—"Tim, you were a beat behind in the entire 'Nutcracker' sequence last night," I was told once, at Radio City—it was impossible for my loose lips not to sputter, and explain: "I had a minor earache and could barely hear the music, and, and, and . . . !" You get the drift.

Luckily, I had a sensitive enough superior who took me aside one day, gently squeezed my shoulder in the manner that says, *You're a young, adorable idiot*, and explained that I never again had to offer a long-winded monologue on why something went wrong, unless he specifically asked. Just, ya know, take the friggin note. (I nodded, and he released my shoulder.)

I've passed that lesson along to every kid I've ever coached on Broadway. Kids are always easier to motivate and notate, by the way, as they generally have fewer hang-ups and fears. They just go for it, and if you tell them you expect them to just "take the note," they nod and go, "Okay!" Refreshing! But people aren't born like this. You've got to model the behavior.

If you find yourself in the position of offering feedback, critiques, advice, or all-out criticism, particularly if it's directed one-on-one, consider preempting the first "note session" with a version of the following: "Look," you'll say, "it's my job to offer you insights into your performance, and thus I will occasionally be riding you to alter certain things about the way you go about your job. There will be times this sucks for both of us, but one thing I can promise you is: I will do my best to never make it personal. Like, at all. It's just literally my gig, just as it's your gig to occasionally be annoyed by me doing my gig." (By now he'll be nodding and laughing and going, "Totally, totally, all good," but don't stop.)

You'll continue: "The one thing I'll ask, just in the interest of time, is that you simply take the note. Just nod, or say the note back to me in your own words, or let me know you've got it in some way unique to you, and we'll be cool. What you never have to do is explain *why*—unless I ask. As in, why something was late, or sloppy, or why your work has gotten unfocused. Unless there's something going on in your life that I need to know—and that's fine, I'm open to whatever—don't worry about offering excuses. Just take the note. We good?" And then he'll be like, "Totally, totally, all good," again, and you can fist-bump and keep walking.

When you're on the receiving end of feedback in your own life, resist the impulse to get defensive. When you give an excuse as to *how* something got off track—other than in cases of an actual mixup or systemic confusion—you can't help but get into a fight. But when you nod and say, "Thanks, I'll remember that and work on it," an amazing thing happens. The energy behind any possible confrontation disappears, *poof*, just like that. Nearly always, it ain't that deep.

By the way, these same principles applied when I began receiving editorial comments on my books. If your editor sees room for improvement in your work, she's usually onto something. It's her job to keep you in line. And to cut your adverbs. Ruthlessly.

43 LIVE IN A SUITCASE

If you've ever packed a bag for longer than a weekend, you know the challenge of boiling down the essentials. Once you get past a toothbrush, a couple changes of clothes, and a travel-size bottle of Jose Cuervo, what's left? What matters? When you learn to live in a suitcase, you also learn what counts—from possessions to, of course, people.

In my mid-twenties I got hired to be the original dance captain on the first national tour of *Spamalot*. Huge opportunity, right? It was an A-list production, with sit-down stints for months at a time in Toronto, Boston, Washington, D.C., and more. But going on the road means you can't take your whole life with you—I had to cram six months into three bags. Brutal! By the end of that tour, I'd changed my views on "stuff" considerably—and valued how few of my physical trappings I actually needed to feel whole.

Living a streamlined lifestyle is easier than ever these days: From photo albums to paperback books to an actual Rolodex that I used to pack (!), nearly everything I stuffed into my third duffel bag would be on my phone now. (With the exception of my lucky teddy bear, who went everywhere with me, and which no app can replace. Ever.) Everything else from back home, from posters I'd bought at

Clear away clutter to make room for the good stuff.

IKEA to a pair of turquoise candlesticks my grandma had given me, had been left in storage when I sublet my New York City studio. By the time I returned home, I was strangely overwhelmed with how much . . . well, junk was there to greet me. (Sorry, Grandma. Still have those candleholders!) I ended up donating five garbage bags of bric-a-brac in order to clear out my own space and make it more hotel-like. (To this day, I miss turndown service and mini-shampoos. And free HBO.)

Now, keep in mind, the Manhattan apartment I came home to was the approximate size of most kitchens in Cincinnati, so any extra space I could carve out wasn't just a premium—it was a luxury. Still, clearing away clutter to make room for the good stuff—like, ya know, other people, and room to think—is what breathing easy is all about, no matter how much square footage you call your own.

So, how can you customize your own space? More important, how can you keep what matters, and whittle down the rest? I'm not suggesting you downsize to a tote bag. Populating your home with mementos that bring to mind happy times and actual accomplishments is a must. And distilling your essentials to the real stuff isn't all that complicated nowadays. When you cut the cable cord and lose the exercise bike (which has, more recently, been used as a sweater drier on laundry day), what you're left with is . . . surprise, yourself! And aren't you sort of great?

The most valuable thing about you is your voice—and I don't mean for singing. You are made up of your thoughts, which become actions. And though the clothes on your back bring comfort and reflect status, they aren't there when the lights go off at night. When you're in the dark, in a hotel room, or your new boyfriend's apartment for the first time, or your own childhood bedroom on a holiday visit home, what you're left with is the way you feel about *you*. Learning to live in a suitcase means figuring out what's unique about yourself, and not the trappings that sometimes obscure what you're really about.

44 GO ON "VOCAL REST"

Much is made of the silly way singers coddle their voices, wrapping scarves around their necks at the first sign of winter, walking around with travel mugs of tea, and popping lozenges like they're mints. Some theatrical roles are so vocally demanding—Evita comes to mind—that, historically, the actors playing them don't even do a full eight performances a week. They take two daylight shows off, and not to party. Presumably, they're drinking more tea than whiskey. Behind the mild drama of "vocal rest"—that is, the practice of not speaking all day, so you can save the good stuff for your performance—is an idea that more of us could build into our everyday lives.

When you walk through the world with a million opinions, but temporarily refrain from voicing them, you hear things differently. You hear *people* in a new way, when you're not busy talking. You realize how few of us actually take the time to reflect and then respond; how we'd rather wait for someone to stop yapping on so that we can yap again ourselves. But when you're speaking, you're not learning.

The pauses between talking are just as important as the talking itself, if not more so. Sometimes nothing is more powerful than the person who keeps completely mum—until he comes up with a whopper of a revelation. It's the most counterintuitive thing, to use

Use silence as a form of quiet strength.

silence as a form of quiet strength. And yet, I've watched many a director cede to an entire room of people, from casting directors to dance assistants, before offering her "take" on something vital, like a casting decision. Inevitably, she'll get her way, as the last person weighing in.

The practice of a non-actor's "vocal rest" might include voicing your opinion only when you've really got something to add to the conversation. It was Abraham Lincoln (or possibly Mark Twain) who said, "Better to remain silent and be thought a fool than to speak out and remove all doubt"—and *Hamilton*'s Aaron Burr who sang, "Talk less, smile more."

Once a week, even if it's just for an hour, notice how differently you communicate if you don't jump in to offer your take on every issue. It drains your batteries to always express your opinions. Dare yourself to remain neutral, and let it manifest as "sitting this one out." A good actor makes something out of every signal he's given. But life isn't an act. It can actually be incredibly restful when you decide to not pick up every single cue the world throws at you.

45 WRITE AN ASPIRATIONAL PLAYBILL BIO

I hate to bring the room down here, but what is the thing you'd like to leave people with, when you make your final exit? Not stage right, but to the Heaviside Layer, or heaven, or wherever it is you think you'll go after taking your last bow. What is it about your life that you'd want people to read about—both your accomplishments and your relationships, and also your quieter pursuits—your day-dreams, your donations, the time you mowed your neighbor's lawn just because. Now pursue that life story, backward. You might call it a future obit. I call it an aspirational *Playbill* bio.

When I first arrived in New York, before I had any significant credits to speak of, I used to fantasize and even write out fake *Playbill* bios about my imagined future self. (Gag, right? But whatever keeps you motivated.) *Playbill* is that old-school magazine with the yellow banner, which they hand out at shows—real shows, the ones that proclaim, *This is the big leagues.* Every member of the company gets a bio, a place to declare: *This is what I've done, world!* Well, younger me would cook up these long-winded fictional bios ("Tim is thrilled to be joining the company of *The Phantom of the Opera* in the title role . . ."), picturing all the shows I'd someday appear in. These bios were epic, containing lessons, quotes from musicals, and self-import-ant thank-yous to the various teachers who'd helped me get "here today"—as if I were anywhere at all but my studio apartment, with no working windows and a shower that always ran cold or colder.

Imagine my mild horror when I actually got hired for my first Broadway show, and was politely informed by the press relations office that I had something like twenty or thirty words for my entire bio. Twenty! My own name took that tally down to eighteen! As I got older and more experienced, my bios grew to fifty or a hundred words—but the sentiment remained the same: How do you sum-marize and pay tribute to the credits and classes and coaches who helped you become who you are today?

Write yourself an aspirational bio—a story about the type of person you want to both be and be known as. Think of it as the best-case bio of a character you'd be proud to know—yourself. The guy or girl who's always cool to Lyft drivers and waiters, and holds doors open for slow people, and picks up litter, even when nobody's looking. Don't necessarily imagine what's going to *seem* impressive to an audience sitting down to read about you. Imagine instead how it would feel to attend your own memorial service, during which a beloved relative steps up to the podium to read this bio aloud, beginning with: "So-and-so was best known for *X* accomplishment—but I want to tell you about all the things she cared for, tenderly, behind the scenes." That's your starting place.

Is this all getting too heavy? If there's one thing musicals have taught me about life and death, it's that they're intertwined; the saddest ballads often have the catchiest melodies. I encourage you not to live your life from one status update to another. Get more holistic. If a thousand strangers glanced at a quick list of all the gifts you had given the world, what would you want them to read? Now write it and live it.

We don't know how much time we've got. It's all a guess. That's the other thing musicals taught me: Your favorite characters can disappear at any moment. In the great *Playbill* bio of the sky, make your twenty words count.

46 TRY TO NAME ALL OF LAST YEAR'S TONY WINNERS

There's a good chance that the award winners of yesterday have already been forgotten today. Seriously. Try to make a list of all of last year's Tony winners, even just the "best actress" list. It's tough, huh? And it isn't just the Tonys. I can never remember who or which movie exactly won an Oscar by about the first Tuesday after the ceremony. It doesn't make these nights unimportant, but it speaks to just how transient it all is. Yes, you should strive for your own accolades—but if your personal version of happiness hinges on rarified pleasures, you're in for an awful lot of tough days.

When I was a kid, the Tony Awards were the single most important night of my life, not counting Christmas and Stephen Sondheim's birthday. After I'd taped the awards (while simultaneously watching them live), I'd pop open a black Magic Marker to scrawl on the outside of the VHS, in all caps: DO NOT RECORD OVER THIS OR YOU WILL DIE. (These words were, of course, empty, as my dear dad "accidentally" taped over the 1994 Tonys with the dang Super Bowl; I allowed him to live after much consideration.) Though these awards held an adorably sacred place in my teen heart, the truth is that not a whole lot of people our there in the Plains states were watching the Tonys with me. It's a rare group, folks. Would I love to win my own Tony someday? You bet. Would 99 percent of the people I meet, on a day-to-day basis, care either way? Not much.

In the Venn diagram of "successful artist" and "successful human," there are many overlaps, including: Listen to whatever kind of drive you have, no matter the insane odds—but also, let go of the results. Or try to.

Half my friends in New York study meditation. One of them even became a famous teacher. Emily flies all over the place, teaching people how to stay still. It all used to make me chortle a bit, till I tried it myself. Forcing oneself to focus and get centered is vital when you live in a town where nobody wants to be average. And yet, if every one of us got a gold star just for waking up, it wouldn't mean anything. If you stick around long enough, however, your own above-average day will come. It just might not manifest the way you originally planned. Plans are funny, that way.

You likely can't name last year's award winners—and, if you can, I'll bet you couldn't tell me who played in the Super Bowl. Even the mightiest honors get swept away in the next breathless news cycle— but don't let that dissuade you from pursuing your own glories, as long as you remember that trophies look great on a mantel, but are only one little part of a big life. Don't live yours for just a single night each year.

Find pleasure and meaning in the quiet days. The ones where the applause has to come from within, for doing the best you could.

47 KNOW THAT YOU'RE BOTH IRREPLACEABLE AND REPLACEABLE

very one of us wants to feel special. We wanna be one-of-a-kind, irreplaceable stars. Unique in ways that aren't threatening to others. And in our own ways, we are. But the truth is, for all the wonders you bring the world . . . you are also somewhat replaceable. We all are. Let this be a guide, not a downer.

I'll never forget the feeling of going back to the Lunt-Fontanne Theatre, right off Times Square, to revisit the company of *The Little Mermaid* months after I'd left the show to pursue an assistant directing opportunity. Right from the start, on the night of my return, something felt "off" about going back. It was *weird* to be entering the theater alongside the audience, and not backstage with my castmates. Well, my former castmates. I was antsy when the house lights went down, and by the time the overture began, my heart was all-out pounding. The "Under the Sea" steel drum percussion played like an old, muscle-memory cue—one that said I should be running around offstage-right, high-fiving my favorite crew guy and singing my "Oohs" and "Ahhs" along with the rest of the fish. When the curtain finally went up at the top of the show, I wanted to shout, "Stop!" Like the whole dang thing couldn't go on unless I was a part of it. Ha. As if.

The truly revelatory moment for me was watching as another actor swam his way onstage, wearing all of "my" costumes—including a blue Lycra bodysuit. Naturally, he performed brilliantly in the role I'd previously considered my own. Hell, he'd been doing it for months now, eight shows a week, with me nowhere in sight. Wow, I recall thinking to myself, *it's like I never even did the show.*

This is why we think of Julie Andrews (and not Mary Martin, who originated the role of Maria) in *The Sound of Music*. Or Audrey Hepburn (and not Julie Andrews) as Eliza Doolittle in *My Fair Lady*. And did you know that Broadway (and TV!) star Sutton Foster started as the *understudy* in *Thoroughly Modern Millie*, before donning the bob-cut hairdo herself and going on to win a sweet little Tony?

News flash: There's always somebody raring to put on your wig, folks.

Realize there's always another person ready, willing, and eager to take over your particular role.

Is this a bit depressing? I hope not too much. The day you realize there's another person ready, willing, and eager to take over your particular "role" is the day you recognize how good you've already got it. That doesn't mean you're some anonymous robot—you bring a certain something to every role you perform, whatever role means to you. But on a hugely populated planet, a whole lot of somebodies out there would happily look at the cards you've been dealt and think, *If only I had it that good.* They'd trade places with you in a moment.

Tomorrow morning, try putting on a slightly different costume. This one will look just like you—same clothes, same hairspray, same smile—but you're gonna wear it a little differently. This time, imagine all the people who'd kill to have your set of setbacks and challenges, and wear that feeling like a custom-made costume. It's called gratefulness—and, unlike a handmade fish suit, it doesn't cost a bundle. In fact, it's free.

48 SCREW UP ONSTAGE, BUT KEEP DANCING

Make a list of all the embarrassing things that could happen to you if you were performing in front of a thousand people. I'll wait. It doesn't need to involve unplanned nudity, by the way—but it should turn your face red. The funny thing is, almost any one of those humiliating things would make for the all-time most memorable performance an audience member had ever seen. Crowds—especially crowds at any live experience—love nothing more than an underdog pulling through. In fact, they clap *harder* when the leading man's fake mustache comes unglued and he *just keeps singing*. Your job is to screw up and keep singing. Not to apologize, but to soldier on.

The master stagecrafter Tommy Tune so keenly understood the audience appeal of onstage mishaps that he actually built "mistakes" into his musicals. It's rumored that in *The Will Rogers Follies*, Tune staged a dialogue sequence so that an actual "actor" dog, who had appeared in an earlier scene, would "accidentally" run across the stage—as if he'd somehow gotten loose backstage and made a mad dash for the footlights. And when did Tune reportedly plan for this nightly interruption to happen? During a quiet scene between two leading actors—who would, during every performance, react as if they hadn't expected little Bowwow to be appearing with them. The female actress would begin laughing, the male actor would "struggle" to keep it together, and sooner or later the audiences would fall all over themselves, going crazy, thinking they were the first people in history to see such an amusing incident. The dog would exit, eventually, and the show would carry on—but the stories those audience members took away lingered far after.

People love slips and blunders; think of all the YouTube videos that have gone viral, and not because they captured a perfect moment in time. A wedding video in which the bride *doesn't* fall into a swimming pool does not get a billion clicks.

Sometimes memorable human mess-ups occur on an even grander stage—and is there a bigger one than the Olympics? If you're a kid who came of age in the nineties, you'll never forget Kerri Strug landing on a broken ankle in order to clinch gold for the American gymnastics team. Would we still be talking about the

'96 games decades later if everything had gone hunky-dory? If Kerri hadn't injured herself moments earlier—and *in spite of it*, soldiered through, and limped her way into glory *and* the hearts of the world? Tens of millions of people from opposing countries were suddenly rooting for the comeback kid. And not despite her having an uphill battle. Because of it.

Theater, above all other arts, provides that coveted feeling of being an insider, because we are literally in the same room as the performers. Mistakes are gonna happen, onstage and in everyday life. More often than not, they're more mortifying to you than to others, so try to find a way to chuckle it off the next time you're not quite "on." Like, you're giving your best man's speech and halfway through you discover your zipper is down? Good. You've just provided the talking points for the evening. Frankly, you've done the room a favor.

Screw up but keep going, and you may be surprised how hard people root for anyone who's rallying for a return to glory. Now zip up your pants and get thee to the open bar.

49 FIND YOUR TRIBE

'm lucky to receive a lot of letters (and emails, and tweets) from young people who identify as LGBTQ+. They seek me out because I've written a bunch of young adult novels, a couple of which feature a young teen auditioning for a fictional Broadway version of *E.T.: The Musical*. Now, you can't write about a kid who's a diehard musical freak without also hinting that he might just grow up to be gay, so those kids who identify with him find me.

There tends to be one overarching theme to all these letters—even when the ages and locations are all over the literal map—and the theme is: *My parents aren't cool with me being a certain way,* whatever that way is, *so what's your advice?* No matter how young that person is, my advice is always the same. Find your tribe.

I wouldn't dare offer something truly prescriptive in my emails back, like: *Move to New York someday! Come play with the rest of us weirdos!* But I do wish that everyone could discover their gang somewhere, the people who *get* them, who accept and validate and don't even blink at their oddities. Whatever your oddities may be—from dressing up like comic book characters to being obsessed with motorcycle repair—there's a place where your thing is everyone's thing. Get to that place, any way you can.

It's a blessing to have the types of parents who brag about you in the family Christmas letter, sure. But if you don't have that inborn support system, you need to build one up, create a scaffolding of help, and hope. One day, your island of misfit toys will begin feeling like the mainland. You deserve that.

When I was in middle school, I spent so much energy zipping from cafeteria table to cafeteria table, trying to impress everybody and make the football players laugh, that I barely had time to eat my pizza bagel. I was desperate to see myself in others, to find other boys who knew every Eponine lyric from *Les Miz*. Eventually I learned that my tribe was way off-campus. We would gather at 2 p.m. every day at an after-school theater program across town that I'd attend three nights a week. If I could just survive from 9 a.m. to 1:30 p.m.—if I could muddle through math and fake my way through French—there was gold on the other side of that rainbow. Or, rather, a rainbow on the other side of the storm.

The best tribes are also where the serious work gets made. Look to the Steppenwolf Theatre Company in Chicago, from which shows

Whatever your oddities—there's a place where your thing is everyone's thing.

like *August, Osage County* burst forth. The team behind that Pulitzer-winning play had been working together for decades—a makeshift family who made stuff. This is to say nothing of all the longtime duos throughout theater history, from Rodgers & Hammerstein to Pasek & Paul. Finding your tribe means developing a shorthand set of customs so you can truly get down and be yourself. Enough with the small talk. Let's think big with our peeps.

There will be growing pains. The moment you realize that there are folks out there who are just like you is also the day you may have outgrown your old tribe. Friend breakups are often harder than romantic breakups. Dare yourself to have the strength of conviction to only make room for people who dovetail with your "I want" song. Life is a journey. Who do you want riding shotgun?

Nah, wait. Life isn't a journey, it's a musical. Choose your costars wisely. Live it up, break into song in the middle of CVS, and find the people who spontaneously add on harmonies without apologizing.

Trust me on this one.

50 LIFE IS NOT A DRESS REHEARSAL

I f you have spent any portion of your life waiting for permission, consider this sentence that permission. Go. Do the thing. You know what "the thing" is, or you wouldn't have kept reading. Commit to living your real life, right now. Not tomorrow. Unless you know something I don't know, you don't get do-overs on earth.

I like to think of life as one very long show with no intermission, during which you're constantly learning about yourself, your own performance, and the vast audience made up of everyone you'll ever meet. And then one day, perhaps with little to no warning, your show is gonna close.

Midway through my high school years, I was on a downward spiral. I'd recast myself in the role of the school's class clown, simultaneously flunking and charming my way through remedial math. Truth is, behind the facade was a lot of fear—about the future and what I might not ever add up to. I figured if I never applied myself at all, I could always look back and say to myself, *Well I coulda been somebody, but I just never tried.* Safer in the shadows, you know? I both wanted desperately to be discovered (as if teenage boys are regularly airlifted from Pennsylvania to Times Square) and also to go utterly unnoticed. I'd lurk in the corner at dance class and never raise my hand to volunteer for solos in choir. This odd timidity was fueled by the strange impression that I'd live forever—that someday, during my presumably long life, I'd wake up . . . ready. Ready to sing out. To step forward.

And then one day my drama club acquaintance, Ellie, was killed in a car accident outside our school. Childhood over—hers and mine. Intertwined with the horror of seeing a fellow teenager lying motionless in an open casket was the realization that my "someday" had arrived. Not the imagined someday, when I'd feel ready, but the day I had to make myself ready. I knew I needed to move myself to the front of dance class, and dare myself to be known. Not just that: to be brave enough to show how eager I was to stop waiting and to start living. Eager has no chill. Eager is vulnerable. Eager is the way forward.

Life is not a dress rehearsal. Until Ellie's death, I had never known somebody during my short but privileged life who had died—not anyone under age eighty, anyway. When Ellie's voice vanished, I somehow in turn found mine; I'd remain the class clown, sure, but I'd try harder, this time not just for me but for Ellie, too. And for anyone whose own experience on Earth was cut tragically short, or who never had the tenacity to try something scary—something she'd most certainly fail at, but had to try anyway. For anyone who never arrived at her someday.

I cannot promise any reader of this book a particular outcome about your own future. I can guarantee, however, that there will be no mythical day when you are suddenly handpicked to play the lead role in your own life. That day already occurred. It's called your birthday, the first one—before cakes and candles, and disappointments. You were born whole and ready to take on the role of your only lifetime.

Start doing things that feel significant and meaningful to you, even if it means occasionally embarrassing yourself. Not just onstage, but everywhere. People tend to regret things they don't do more than what they attempt and suck at. Sociological fact! Crack on a high note at karaoke. At least you'll have an anecdote afterwards. But if you sit back and never get up, you'll be self-diagnosing a terminal illness known as Wondering. The symptoms of Wondering include: stressing out about who you could have been, what you could have accomplished, where you could have lived out your happiest days.

Every breakup, makeup, and night spent sobbing over the hot boy in the cast—the one who always gets to play the lead and never seems to notice you in the background? It's all part of the show—the good, the bad, and the hilarious. Start living your life as if the finale might be coming soon, because someday you'll be right. You'll want to look back knowing that you left your desires and attempts, full-hearted and half-accomplished, center stage for the world to witness, instead of locked up tight inside your head.

Wondering only has one cure. It's called Doing.

So go do, and see. And live.

ACKNOWLEDGMENTS

The author wishes to thank his theater teachers, mentors, dance partners, collaborators, ex-boyfriends (nearly all of them), current boyfriend, and especially students he's been lucky enough to be inspired by along the way. Also, thanks to his dad, for paying for private voice lessons, and his mom, for driving him. Grateful acknowledgement to everyone at Hachette and Running Press, particularly his editor, Jennifer Kasius. And special thanks to Brenda Bowen, agent and chief advisor.